THE
MEDITERRANEAN
LOVE PLAN

OTHER BOOKS AUTHORED OR CO-AUTHORED BY STEPHEN ARTERBURN

THE MEDITERRANEAN LOVE PLAN

SEVEN SECRETS TO LIFELONG PASSION IN MARRIAGE

STEPHEN AND MISTY ARTERBURN
WITH BECKY JOHNSON

ZONDERVAN

The Mediterranean Love Plan
Copyright © 2017 by Steve Arterburn

Requests for information should be addressed to:
Zondervan, *3900 Sparks Dr. SE, Grand Rapids, Michigan 49546*

Library of Congress Cataloging-in-Publication Data

ISBN 978-0-310-33546-7 (hardcover)

ISBN 978-0-310-34871-9 (international trade paper edition)

ISBN 978-0-310-35033-0 (audio)

ISBN 978-0-310-33416-3 (ebook)

Published in association with the literary agency of Wordserve Literary Group, Ltd., www.wordserveliterary.com.

Cover design: Curt Diepenhorst
Cover photo: © Mv_Jamsey/iStock
Interior design: Denise Froehlich

First printing February 2017 / Printed in the United States of America

CONTENTS

INTRODUCTION

MONOTONOUS MARRIAGE OR A *GRANDE AMORE?*

I'm a radio show host on a call-in show called *NewLife Live,* on which people call in to tell me and my cohosts (and the world) their private and most painful problems. Perhaps not surprisingly, most of these calls revolve around how difficult it is to be passionate about the people they love or used to love or are supposed to love (not to mention all the destructive things they've done once their love began to fade). I also get plenty of calls from singles searching for that one perfect person who will solve all their problems, cure all their ills, and heal all their wounds (or so they wish).

Then there are hundreds who found and married the Love of Their Life and had a romantic time in which they flirted wildly or made passionate love on a whim. They may recall running along some beach, laughing, kissing, caught up in the beauty of sea and sand and each other. But then work, kids, the pressures of life, and plain old neglect took over, and what once was all a-sizzle is now starting to fizzle. Sadly, this is often the way love goes if we simply let our relationships run the natural course. However, wise couples can create conditions that keep their passion percolating. Which is why Misty and I wrote this book. We have a heart to see marriages overcome the depressing stats that say romance starts fading soon after two starry-eyed lovers say "I do."

It is true, however, that the neurotransmitters of "falling in love" last an average of a whopping six whole months. Research has shown that once the brain's supply of natural love potion runs out, the honeymoon ends. Most couples go back to focusing primarily on work, adapt to mundane routines in their newly mortgaged home, and soon morph into parents who lose sleep and somehow eventually lose touch with each other (in every meaning of that word). Then one day they wake up feeling lonelier in their marriage than they ever felt as a single person. They're adrift, wondering who they are, who they married, and how something so passionately promising could have turned out so painfully bland. Lifeless. Loveless. Sexless.

Without knowing how to handle the inevitable disappointments and challenges, they find that the Three C's of misery—criticism, complaining, and comparison—tend to come marching in. The changes are so extreme that the couple feel stunned. Hopelessness replaces happiness, and horrible is the only word to describe the disaster. When I see couples like this, I can't help but think of accident victims. One or both appear to be in a state of shock and in need of rescue. I call these severe cases radical flips. The husband and wife feel almost unrecognizable to each other as the marriage morphs into an emotional war zone.

But even these extreme cases are not hopeless, as long as the couple call for the right kind of help as early as possible.

Other couples don't experience a radical flip as much as they do an effortless flop. These partners settle into comfortable routines and have plain vanilla marriages that are not particularly painful but are more like business partnerships with a goal to "get 'er done" (whatever the "er" is on their to-do list). They are no longer a passionate couple with shared dreams of a long, happy future.

Instead they've become detached from each other's hearts, living with sad regrets and dreams that have come undone.

- "We love each other after all these years. We're good friends. But the spark? Romance? Flirting? A honeymoon memory that faded a long time ago."
- "After being up all night with a new baby, we both still get very

excited about going to bed with each other—to do nothing but *sleep*."

In a scene from *Under the Tuscan Sun*, two young lovers ask for their parents' blessing to marry. The girl's mother, disappointed in her own marriage, urges her daughter not to saddle up for life with her poor Polish suitor. She tells her daughter that love is the stuff of fairy tales, that true love is a fantasy, implying she should look for a husband with wealth and stability instead.

But just then the old grandmother intervenes, declaring with emotion, "I had a *grande amore*—a great love! Your father. And I will never forget!"

Sigh.

Is a *grande amore* possible in today's fast-paced Western culture? Don't most couples eventually stay together out of obligation rather than great passion? Is a lifelong love affair the stuff of days gone by or fairy tales and romance novels?

Well, it all depends.

It depends on whether you are willing to do something besides simply calling it a life and waiting out the clock. If both of you are not proactive about passion, I can guarantee that one day you'll be pulling up your Depends and wondering, "Where did we go wrong? When did the romance die?" If, that is, you are even still together.

Does anyone really have a marriage that grows more romantic as the years go by, a powerful and stunning union that lasts forever? If you are willing to change the way you think, risk trying some of the suggestions we make (even if they're a bit outside of your comfort zone), then I believe the answer is a passionate yes! The million-dollar question is, "How, exactly, do we make the fairy tale come true? How do we keep the spark not just *going* but *growing* and *glowing* for decades?"

So glad you asked.

There are hundreds of books on communication in marriage and hundreds more about spicing up your sex life. But realistically, who wants to communicate with someone who has become bored and boring or who has become closed off to their own desires? Who wants to have sex with someone who is doing their marital duty, checking you off their list? The truth is, no book can fix a marriage if one or both people in the marriage have lost their zest for life and their commitment to make romance a top priority.

After decades of studying marriage, I realized there is a dearth of books about how to live sensually and passionately, in all of life, with your mate. Romance is much more than a date night or a week away. To have a passionate love life, you need two people who are sensually in love with life and each other. Imagine taking out the dream you had of a lifelong romance and dusting it off like a painting you've stored away on a shelf. Now imagine taking this painting with you on a trip to the Mediterranean, where you meet passionate artistic masters like Da Vinci and Picasso and Michelangelo. They are delighted with your painting, but they also point out where it needs a splash of light, where the colors need to be more intense, and show you how to add beautiful details— pointers that make your painting almost come to life. With the help of the masters, your painting is now so vivid that you can almost hear the music from the sidewalk cafe and smell the flowers from its window boxes. Now imagine stepping into this painting, together, where you continue creating rapturous moments and romantic memories that will never fade.

In the pages to come, I hope to help you and your spouse create a vision for a passionate life and marriage, somewhat like that painting. This may mean dusting off an old vision for a romantic marriage that you once held dear or creating a fresh vision for what a fun, intimate marriage can look like. And we'll go to the Art of Romance School with the masters of passion, taking love lessons from the Mediterranean, where the experts at living more sensuously will help us add light and color and beauty to our relationships. All with the reachable goal of helping your marriage come alive!

We will share fascinating research on the science-based secrets of creating passion, drawn from five of the most famously romantic countries along the Mediterranean Sea: Greece, France, Italy, Spain, and Israel.

Granted, the Mediterranean countries may not do everything well (like getting anything done on time or launching adult males from their mama's kitchens), but they know about passion.

The countries that produced Michelangelo, Socrates, *Les Misérables*, opera, Tuscan sunlight, fabulous wine, creamy fettuccini, steamy shots of rich espresso, the Song of Solomon, and more have a long history of passionate romantics. About this subject, they are the world's experts. From the Spaniards, men might learn how to "really, really love a woman" so that your wife blesses the day she was born female. And a wise wife can inspire her husband to declare, "I. Am. Spartacus!" with a few lessons from some of the wise, secure, passionate women of the Mediterranean.

American couples (Misty and I among them!) pay good money to go on Mediterranean cruises and trips to Italy or Paris, usually with one major goal in mind: to fall more deeply in love with life and each other. To remember romance. To stop and smell the roses and olive gardens and garlicky pizza and a fine Bordeaux. Instinctively we know where to go to restart our sensual engines. And it isn't Montreal or Hong Kong or London. It's Italy, France, Greece, and Spain. And when we hunger for more passion in our spiritual lives, we book trips to the Holy Land, to walk where biblical stories come to life. There is something magical, mystical, and marvelous about the countries along that sparkling azure sea.

Misty and I have a houseful of kids—ranging from kindergarten to college age—so we've had our share of pizza delivered to the front door, then devoured in front of the television with the whole fam watching a football game or a Disney movie.

And every time I open up a box of pizza and smell the aroma of fresh bread, garlic, and tomatoes, I'm transported to a moment in time with my lovely wife.

Several years ago, after a long time of saving up for a Mediterranean vacation, we found ourselves sitting on a beach in Naples, Italy. The sun was high, but the heat was relieved by a cool breeze off the Mediterranean Sea, that gorgeous blue water I had seen, until then, only in photos and videos. But at that moment, there it was, as stunning as I had dreamed it would be. The water was like blue liquid velvet rolling onto the warm sand where we sat, cross-legged, eating what could not be described merely as pizza. This "food of the gods" drooped in our hands so that we had to fold the fresh bread to take a bite; rich olive oil mingled with fresh tomato sauce dripped and drooled from the corners of our mouths. Every sense was alive in that moment, and in that space we saw each other free of any flaws and defects. We didn't *choose* to kiss each other, we were *compelled* into a kiss, into one of those kisses where you can't get enough of each other, a kiss that lingers, that scintillates, melts you into one.

I've seen hundreds of romantic films, and all I can say is, in that moment, along the Mediterranean, Misty and I *were* the movie. All the elements that evoke passion were present: the amazing aroma from the pizza, the gentle breeze on our faces, the warm sand under our feet. When we finished eating, we walked into the cool and splendorous water of the Mediterranean, laughing as it splashed up and around our legs.

Time seemed to stop on this warm afternoon, and we felt filled to overflowing with love for our lives and for each other. Even as I write this, the memory and feelings of love and connection to Misty are bubbling up all over again.

This is what passionate memories do to us, don't they? They carry us down rabbit trails to sweet moments in our shared history. And by reliving them in our mind, we are blessed anew with sensual feelings for each other in the present.

In the last decade or more, a slew of books have sung the praises of Mediterranean diets. But what the diet books don't say is that health, happiness, and longevity is not just about eating more vegetables doused with olive oil and downed with merlot. It is also about living in a culture that prioritizes and emphasizes passion, romance, beauty, and sensuality as a normal way of being. Studies show that beyond food and exercise, there is another common thread among people who live long: they love well and are loved back in return.[1]

If we want more *joie de vivre*, more of *la dolce vita* in our marriages, why not study the masters of passion? Not only to spice up our relationships but also to relight the flame of passion for life itself. In this book, I have pulled together the best research, interviews, and ideas from the world's most romantic countries; I will also share how Misty and I live out the principles of passion in our everyday lives, keeping our love fresh and alive, even with a houseful of kids and a to-do list that never ends.

In the next chapter, I will unveil how the seven mysteries of ultimate intimacy from ancient cultures along the Mediterranean Sea can help couples create conditions for vibrant passion and rich connection. These secrets will help your love intensify with time rather than die a slow death. If you and your partner apply them, I promise you will be well on your way to experiencing a truly *grande amore*.

A quick note about the voice in this book. Misty and I reminisced, discussed, and wrote together; however, we found it unwieldy to switch voices back and forth. So to keep things simple, we chose to write in my voice. Just know that my insightful wife contributed her thoughts, memories, and ideas to what you are about to read.

Unthinkably good things can happen even late in the game. It's such a surprise.

—FRANCES MAYES, *UNDER THE TUSCAN SUN*

CHAPTER I

THE SEVEN MEDITERRANEAN SECRETS TO PASSION

Have you never met a woman who inspires you to love?
Until your every sense is filled with her? You inhale her.
You taste her. You see your unborn children in her eyes
and know that your heart has at last found a home.

—*DON JUAN DEMARCO*

In the film *Don Juan DeMarco*, a middle-aged psychiatrist (played by Marlin Brando) is asked to help what appears to be a delusional young man (played by Johnny Depp) who wears a mask and claims to be *the* Don Juan, the world's greatest lover. The therapist tries to get the young man to, well, snap out of it! Be sane, be normal! Whether this Don Juan's identity is false or real becomes of less consequence as the movie progresses, the therapeutic tables are turned, and the incurable romantic is suddenly teaching the practical psychiatrist about the Spanish art of seduction and love.

Over weeks of therapy sessions, the aging psychiatrist becomes more and more influenced by the romantic philosophies of his client. He finds himself, at home, slowly awakening to his senses and becoming a more attentive and passionate lover to his oft-neglected but beautiful wife. By the movie's close, we see the therapist twirling and waltzing with his wife as he walks with her along the beach on the island of Eros, having blossomed into a man renewed to the passion of life itself, a passion ignited as he romanced his woman.

Men, I would love for the book you are holding to ignite your inner (monogamous) Don Juan. And women, I want you to fully embrace your womanhood with the man in your life. I want you both to start living sense-drenched, passionate lives when apart and together.

I have to admit, it takes some focused effort to learn and practice the art of living and loving at a high level. Nothing kills romance and passion quite like allowing a marriage to simply unfold naturally. If you aren't proactive about applying the secrets of passion to your marriage, every day, it won't be long before your relationship is on autopilot: both of you prioritizing your separate to-do lists rather than carving out time to linger and celebrate your love together.

You may not find yourself in a monotonous marriage overnight; it happens slowly, bit by bit. But if you leave your marriage untended, you could wake up one day and (insert loud yawn) both feel bored at best, trapped at worst.

You have to be conscious about bringing out your inner Don Juan (or Zorba the Greek or Sophia Loren or Valentino or Juliet or Helen of Troy or Pepe Le Pew). As one old Mediterranean adage declares, "Love is like good bread. It has to be made new every day." That said, what exactly do great romantics do to keep aflame their zest for life and their desire for intimacy?

I'd like to begin answering that question by sharing a landmark study on the subject of ecstasy (the emotion, not the drug).

SEVEN SECRETS TO A MORE PASSIONATE RELATIONSHIP

In the early 1960s, writer and researcher Marghanita Laski conducted what would become a classic study on the subject of ecstasy.[1] She discovered that there were certain elements surrounding experiences of passionate joy and romantic love. They occurred so often, she began calling them triggers to ecstasy.

Among the triggers to ecstatic experiences were

- being in nature
- observing art or listening to music
- discovery of new knowledge
- beauty
- spiritual and religious experiences
- rhythmic movement
- sexual love and tender touch

From my own research and observation, other common prompts to passion include

- playfulness, humor, and laughter
- intimate, soul-satisfying connection
- a meal prepared and eaten with mindfulness and love

By incorporating more of these God-given pleasures into our daily lives, we become more sensual, happy people. And when a couple both encourages and regularly shares together many of these passion triggers, or what I prefer to call intimacy inducers, romance continues to blossom.

Contrast the practices listed above to what we see, too often, in modern American marriages: faces glued to smartphones, hands on computer game consoles, husbands in man caves watching sports from their Barcaloungers, women so crazy-busy that they've lost touch with their own emotions, children who watch their parents live parallel lives rather than living intertwined and deeply connected lives through intimate romance and affectionate love. My heart aches for so many couples in trouble, who are daily weighing the question that divides and decays any relationship: "Should I stay or should I go?" It is no wonder that we have lost our passion and need a plan to find it, nurture it, and experience romantic love in all of its mysterious grandeur.

By combining, grouping, and distilling what Laski learned about triggers to ecstasy with the practices that lead to passion in the world's most romantic countries, I have come up with the following Seven Secrets of Passion, unveiled here for you.

1. *The Secret of Attunement.* Tuning in to one another, getting in sync regularly, using all of our senses.
2. *The Secret of Playfulness.* Being fully engaged in things both spouses find that bring a sense of childlike fun and joy to the marriage.
3. *The Secret of Savoring Food.* Cooking and/or sharing a romantic meal together can intensify and enrich the experience of being together, in surprising ways.
4. *The Secret of Enjoying Beauty.* Surrounding ourselves with beauty elevates and inspires our senses and brings out the romantic in all of us.
5. *The Secret of Creativity.* Engaging in creative arts or projects or exciting adventures together turns on the neurotransmitters that support powerful romantic connections and intimate partnership.
6. *The Secret of Health and Longevity.* Staying healthy together through a naturally active and balanced lifestyle leads to more fun in the bedroom as well, lasting into old age.
7. *The Secret of Blending the Sacred and the Sexual.* Couples who naturally and successfully weave their spiritual connection to God with their human desire for closeness and oneness take their marriage to the realm of ultimate intimacy. A shared, sacred purpose also magnifies passion for living and love for each other.

SIDE NOTE: IT TAKES TWO TO TANGO

Though one person applying these principles can become more passionate and have some influence over their partner, a great love requires two people going all in to make their marriage the most passionate it can be. One person can certainly instigate and help get the romance dominoes falling, but because marriage is a two-party invention, one person trying alone cannot create true intimacy.

So I want to say here that if your mate is caught in one of the Four Deadly A's—abuse, addiction (be it drugs, alcohol, porn, food, shopping, gambling, or something else), abandonment, or adultery—you will need a professional counselor who's an expert in helping you navigate these potentially marriage-eroding issues. (In fact, you may want to consider beginning with a NewLife Intensive Marriage Transformation Weekend.) Deeply ingrained personality disorders (such as borderline or narcissistic personality disorder) or Asperger's syndrome or a mental illness (such as bipolar disorder or schizophrenia) can also be serious challenges or even roadblocks to a passionate, intimate marriage. Past sexual abuse may also need to be handled with tender loving care and the guidance of experts who understand the unique path required for recovery.

These are complex issues that no marriage book alone can solve. As much as I'd like to say that one person's love can conquer all ills in a marriage, I cannot. Intimacy ("into-me-see") requires two people who both desire closeness and passion in their marriage. They may not be experiencing it, but they both want it. Some issues, however, so erode a marriage that intimacy cannot happen unless and until the broken foundations of safety, trust, and commitment are rebuilt with expert help and support. So get any professional help you need to repair any cracks in your relational foundation, and use this book as a resource to start adding positive, intimacy-building activities back into your marriage.

Now that I have met my professional duty and responsibility to tell you that this book is not the way to solve all problems in marriage, I want to counter that with another vital piece of reality. The ideas and dreams presented in this book could be the trigger for the complete reimagining of your marriage. An unforgettable moment, an unexpected attempt at romance, may be just the spark needed to ignite the fire of change and transformation. You may be surprised at how applying just one or two of these Mediterranean secrets of romance can get you out of a relational rut, just as they've worked for me and Misty.

At one point in our marriage, Misty and I fell into one of those relational spirals in which we were constantly stepping on each other's toes, and being together started to feel like work. We both ached from the pain of living together, but we were feeling isolated emotionally. So we did something radical. We packed up our resentment and bitterness, left the kids with trusted family and friends, then spent a week alone together in a beautiful spot away from work, laptops, TV, and cell phones. (There was a local phone by which our family could reach us in case of emergency, but that's it.) Once we were truly away from it all, without distractions, we were able to apply several of the secrets to romance that we share in this book, including slowing down our life to the speed of each other's heartbeat, giving our marriage the time and space for us to get in sync and attuned again. (See chapter 2 for more about attunement, a powerful ingredient of passion.)

We arrived in deep despair. Before we left the island, we were bonded back into the marriage we had experienced before we started subtly detaching, the passionate marriage we are experiencing still. There is no marriage on earth that doesn't need the occasional tune-up (or overhaul). Thankfully, before this getaway, we were familiar with the relational tools to mend and enhance our marriage. But what we needed at this point was to stop the world, slow down, and apply these secrets once again, in a concentrated week of healing, connection, and fun. It worked like a miracle.

Also, I want to say that you can certainly explore and apply the mysteries of the Mediterranean to your own life to get back in touch with the passionate joy of living, whether or not your mate participates. For those of you who are dating or looking for a mate, this book will help you become the most passionate person you can be. And it will help you spot a partner who has qualities that contribute to a long-term marriage full of playfulness, intimacy, and romance.

Finally, passion can take on many faces during times of illness or crisis, or the birth of a baby, or life with toddlers. To an exhausted mother, the ultimate intimacy inducer may be a husband who is willing to take the night shift with the newborn. When a mate is battling any kind of illness, from the flu to cancer, romance will look less erotic and more like tender loving care. When either or both of you are facing a crisis—from a dying parent to a teen on drugs—the face of passion will look more like *com*passion. Passion embraces all the senses and emotions of the human experience, of which sexuality is only one. It's an important one, no doubt, but cut each other lots of slack when one of you is going through a rough patch. Ask your ailing, hurting, or exhausted partner, "What can I do to help?" or "What do you need?" or "What would feel good right now?" and honor their requests. Allow romance and passion to take on new meanings that will deepen your love and intimacy, even when life hurts.

Throughout this book, we'll mention movies and characters, books and quotes. Some of these films or books and characters are obviously morally flawed. So we're not endorsing or condoning plot lines that glorify things like promiscuity, but we will be focusing on scenes that vividly illustrate one of the secrets to passion. Our goal is to notice and capture these elements of passion and bring them into committed marriage. So we ask for your grace and understanding: keep the pointers about passion; toss out plot lines or character flaws that are less than God's ideal for marriage.

Finally, we will be giving you more information and ideas in the following chapters than any couple can possibly employ in a short amount of time. As you read, you'll find yourselves drawn to a few ideas that spark your interest or feed your soul. Make note of these; in fact, read the book with a highlighter or pen if possible and mark the thoughts and ideas that most speak to you, perhaps sections that give you a flutter of joy or hope in your stomach, or a quote that brings a tear to your eye. Start by applying the suggestions that most tug at your heart, and don't get overwhelmed, thinking you've got to somehow do everything we suggest in this book, all at once. We hope this will be a book you can keep on your bookshelf and turn to, time and again, in months and years to come when you need a passion booster or two.

And now, without further ado, let's uncover the mysteries that prompt passion, create the conditions for closeness, and bring a renewed sense of romance into your marriage!

———————————◆———————————

Love withers with predictability; its very essence is surprise and amazement. To make love a prisoner of the mundane is to take its passion and lose it forever.

—LEO BUSCAGLIA

CHAPTER 2

THE SECRET OF ATTUNEMENT

If there is a country that seems to have it all, it is Italy. The majesty of Roman architecture, the lush, rolling countryside, dotted with olive orchards and vineyards. And the aromas! The pure, fresh air coming off the sea, the ever-present scents pouring from homes and cafes, where someone is always baking or stewing or stirring up something that will taste better than you can imagine. Everywhere you look in Italy, there is a scene worthy of a painting or just one more photo. No matter how you try to capture the beauty of Italy—with paintbrush or camera—there is no substitute for being there, in the flesh, all your senses alive with its resplendence.

If, that is, you are actually there when you go there.

The truth is, you can be in Italy and miss Italy. You can be on a tour bus, speeding over asphalt, catching blurred glimpses of scenery from the window, while you are constantly distracted by the noise and chatter of other passengers. You can be in the most beautiful place in the world, anywhere in the world, and because of worries or distractions that pull at your mind, you can miss the glory of being fully present for wonder.

In the same way, we can miss the glorious beauty of our mates when we don't slow down, turn off the distractions, and tune in to each other with all our senses.

Thankfully, when Misty and I were able to go on a long-saved-for and much-anticipated trip to the Mediterranean, we took the time needed to get away from crowds and become fully attuned, almost feeling one with the land. We immersed ourselves in the people, the slower pace, and all we could absorb from the culture. We were together in Pisa, Naples, Palermo, Rome, and other beautiful locales, and we didn't miss any detail of their centuries-old culture. We luxuriated in every experience. In addition, we felt we were one with each other. It was a rare and precious moment in time when we were able to turn aside from all distractions back home in Middle America and tune in to the sights, sounds, smells, tastes, touch of the beautiful Mediterranean—and to each other.

As that great Italian crooner Dean Martin sang, "Memories are made of this."

But eventually we had to come home again, as every tourist does. For a while, the memory of a slower pace, of being fully relaxed and present for each other, lingered. But not for long. No matter how sweet, there is no memory strong enough to totally change how we function together back home, day after day. You can, however, choose to bring home the essence of what you experienced elsewhere and apply it to your marriage, often, and watch your relationship slowly blossom with passion. The essence of what Misty and I experienced in Italy was the secret of attunement, though at the time I had no clue what the word *attunement* even meant.

I was a music major in college, so I knew about tuning a piano so that the keys would play notes in harmony. This is a pretty good picture of what attunement means in relationships. It is the ability to tweak your focus until it is in sync, or in harmony, with the person you love.

This concept has been the ultimate challenge for my scattered, fast-running brain. I am a multidecade veteran of the Attention Deficit Disordered War on Relationships. If you only knew how hard I have fought to achieve deep human connection. That connection thing I'd heard so much about was not easy to attain, and once I got it, it felt impossible to sustain for long. In fact, both of us struggled to maintain a close connection, but for differing reasons.

In my case, ADHD produces an internal disorderly conduct, so it is never easy for me to get focused and stay in tune. For people who don't have ADHD, let me try to describe what it's like for our runaway-brain types. Imagine trying to have a conversation with your wife, only your hair is on fire, burning overhead. While you are trying to intently listen to her, look for nuances in her expression, and be sensitive to any emotional gradation, all you see is the flames from your hair reflected in her eyes. You try to focus on her words; you nod, respond. Then brush away burning ashes from your head. You tell yourself, "Focus, focus, focus," but you smell burning flesh. Still you nod, acknowledge her valuable input, ask to hear more (keep your eyes from squinting in the smoke), focus, listen harder, more nodding, loving, responding. But while she is talking, you are waiting for the moment when you can finally stick your head in a bucket of water. It took such a gargantuan effort to control your brain-on-fire while practicing your deep-listening skills! At certain times, that is what staying attuned is like for me. However, if I fail to attune because I am focusing more on the forest fire of thoughts in my head than on my wife's heart, we both pay a price.

Have you ever trusted someone with a vulnerable piece of your heart, said something that meant a great deal to you, and then got what felt like an obligatory and brief response as they turned the conversation to something that seemed to interest them more? We have all experienced this; Misty and I have done it to each other. But the more skilled I get at harnessing my runaway "let's fight that fire!" thoughts, the better I am at attunement.

I have pursued every resource available to tend to my adult ADHD, and not only has my effort to get help for my struggles with focus been helpful for me, but it has also meant so much to Misty.

I'm a long way from having reached perfect *atuno-matata*, but I am upping my skills in focused listening, better able to mirror Misty's responses with thoughtful replies, trying to look for and read Misty's facial cues and linger with her on one subject a little longer. As the saying goes, the struggle is real, but I know that if I want to experience back at home all that Misty and I felt in Italy, I have to conquer attunement—my final frontier of intimate connection.

Many years ago, John F. Kennedy spoke the words, "We choose to go to the moon." Remember, when he said this, it sounded like something out of a sci-fi novel to American ears. We have more technology today in our smartphones than they had in the entire space program in the early sixties. Still, Kennedy declared what was not yet into being. "We choose to go to the moon."

In a similar declaration of faith, I said to myself, "I choose to attune." And trust me, with the short supply of skills I had to work with, I might as well have said, "I am going to the moon."

But Misty and I wanted nothing more than to experience marital oneness, and we were willing to do whatever it took. Something amazing happens when, from the very depths of our soul, we are ready for change. As we humbly invite new possibilities and ways of thinking into our lives, we miraculously begin to change. If a guy with ADHD like me can practice focus and connection, then I believe anyone who is willing can do this.

Now I want Misty to speak to the issue of attunement in her own words, as her struggles to attune have been different from mine. I believe many of you will relate to her challenges.

———————————

(Misty) A challenge I face every day is the practice of keeping my heart soft and open, even in the face of fears and my tendency toward self-protection. Walling off is a "skill" I developed during a childhood in which healthy boundaries were often abandoned in the family I loved so dearly. My sisters and I frequently invaded each other's space without warning in our small house, where personal territory was at a premium. Often we said what we felt, when we felt it, at the intensity with which we felt it, putting it out there without edit or thoughtfulness. I learned to get bigger and louder and more fierce in the face of perceived threat. As close as we sisters were, and as much as we loved each other, in times of conflict there was a struggle inside me. Those times were chaotic, intense, and frightening, and I compensated with the best survival skills I could summon at the time: being on edge, hypervigilant, ready to react, defend, and protect at all times. I realize now that this skill set is common to a lot of us who grew up in homes with high conflict and few boundaries. However, these very skills that helped us navigate our chaos as children no longer serve us in adulthood and can undermine connection and the intimacy we want in a healthy marriage.

All relationships come with ups and downs, times of sweet connection and times of hurt, misunderstandings, and disconnection. But entering into a normal marriage with normal ups and downs with a hypervigilant chip on the shoulder can be a recipe for trouble. A simple disagreement or small annoyance may turn instead into a major conflict.

When it comes to attunement with Steve, I must first practice overall centeredness and connection with God. Attuned to God's love for me and his covering over me, I practice trusting him in my daily life. When I am secure in that relationship, when I am steady and grounded in his love and care for me, I am less apt to react from fear or perceived threat in any situation, and certainly when it comes to my husband. In those moments when I am ready to fire in reaction toward Steve, the best action I can take is to pause. Take a deep breath. Often I will quickly pray the Serenity Prayer and create a buffer zone before I respond. God is meeting me in that pause. And in turn, I am meeting Steve.

Each day presents an opportunity for me to shut down and close off my heart, offended or wounded, hardening the shell around me, then acting in reactionary ways, creating wounds and hurt in my husband, the one I love and yearn to be close to. Instead I can take the opportunity to practice opening my heart, holding it open, even when I have to pry it open with a crowbar to get a sliver more of openness, so that I might move toward my husband rather than moving away. It is difficult for me to do this. I want to react. I want to judge and teach him how to live. My natural response is to want to control outcomes. I can deceive myself, thinking, "If I just explain the situation 'this way' to Steve, maybe things will change. Or if I explain it to him once more, with extra feeling, it might do the trick. If I slam a door loud enough, perhaps that will create the change I want."

Yet God continues gently teaching me that my knee-jerk reactions are counterproductive. They are not helping me or Steve or our marriage. So I am learning and doing the scary thing, the counterintuitive thing: reaching out to Steve with an open heart when what I want to do most is to shut down or run. I will say again, this is not easy for me. I have to gather all my courage to lean in toward my husband when my old reactionary habits are bidding me, "Wall off."

It may take everything I have within me to become the listener in that moment, instead of the speaker. To seek to understand before seeking to be understood. But here's the headline: every time I am able to slow down the pace from my side of the street, get out of my reactionary zone, and look for my spouse's real need during a conflict, we get to the heart of the matter much more gently and much more quickly. I believe that many women reading this, especially those who did not feel relationally safe as a child, will understand. Keeping my heart open requires staying in my adulthood—resting in my connection with God, remembering I have the choice to respond thoughtfully rather than react automatically.

Attunement means I have empathy for my spouse. I can see his joy over something at work, and I can rejoice with him. I can notice that he's looking a little down today and check in on him gently. I can see he is upset and not lose myself in it. I can contain his emotional spouting, because I hurt for him, and I can transcend being offended, for the larger goal of holding his heart in his pain. It means I can understand where he's coming from; I may not like it, but I know that what he really needs more than a lecture from me is a nap. Or a meal. It means when I wake up earlier than he does, I will close the door quietly to promote his sleep. I am in tune with his needs, while simultaneously in tune with mine. And he is aware of me, and supporting me too, in all the same ways.

(Steve) Our marriage has afforded us the environment to heal old wounds and learn new ways of being in relationship. Attunement requires two people who are willing to perceive each other, and truly care, in order to connect. If intimate connection doesn't come naturally to you, don't despair. Get any help you need from counselors or wise mentors, and then make regular time and space for practice and daily attunement. What we prioritize will grow and blossom. This is a lifelong adventure in understanding one another, staying open, and reaching for humility. Reaching for each other. Creating attunement and connection is thrilling when achieved. Joy-filling, awe-inspiring, love-growing marriage is available for all who participate.

Now Misty and I have our own Mediterranean moments of attunement every day. We are tracking together at a deep and soulful level, and we don't have to pay big bucks to visit another country to experience this bliss.

Almost every night possible in our marriage, after we put the younger kids to bed, we spend a good length of time together alone in our big bathtub, sharing experiences from the day and the feelings that have arisen from them. In these moments, we have planned for the future and dreamed up ideas to try to change the world. But mostly we are just fully there *with* each other and *for* each other long enough that we become attuned, to a degree that I never thought possible. This daily practice, sacred to us now, has been a superglue holding us together when it felt like the world, the flesh, and even the Devil (it seemed at times) wanted to rip us apart. For us, the place we often attune best has turned out to be in our big, two-person bathtub.

Aside from the warmth of the water, which helps us relax and be fully present for each other, an interesting dynamic is created by sharing time together in this way. Just the sheer physical vulnerability leads to significant emotional vulnerability as well. Very important in these moments for us is the level of safety and trustworthiness we must provide for each other. Being in each other's presence, naked and facing one another, submerged and talking, is a graduate-level course in trust, acceptance, intimacy, and transparency.

The perimeter of the bathtub is a convenient boundary, creating a space only for us, where no one else has access or the ability to disrupt. It is our place together, and ours alone. It is an interesting experience, all these years, the thousands of times we've held our nightly "meetings," as we call them. We have laughed in our tub together, cried and shared deep sorrows; we have argued, discussed the calendar, held each other in silence, and yes at times launched toward our bedroom.

With all our hearts, Misty and I want to see other couples discover and practice the art of attunement. The bathtub has been our sanctuary together, but no worries if you aren't bath people. Just find a quiet place where you can meet every day for at least twenty minutes, tune out the world, and tune in to each other. It could be your bedroom, a porch swing, a path in the park, opposite ends of your sofa, or a cozy kitchen nook—it doesn't matter where as long as it is special to you, private, and relaxing. (If you have kids, it helps to teach them the boundary not to interrupt at this time, or just enjoy this time together as soon as they've gone to bed.)

I am so proud and happy to say that even though our life is beyond full and requires hard work from both of us, our marriage now often plays like a finely tuned Steinway. I've spent a lot of time traveling in my life. This past year was the final year of Women of Faith, a conference event I started two decades ago. Their Farewell Tour was special, and Misty and I both felt that I needed to be with the speakers I'd come to love and admire, to celebrate the miraculous blessing the Women of Faith conferences have been to more than five million women, and this one very fortunate man. But I have been home now, without traveling, for a long while, and it has been wonderful. On several occasions, Misty has caught me standing and staring in the midst of our family, watching them do what families do. "What are you thinking about?" she asked in one of these moments.

I smiled at her, my heart full, my eyes moist, and said, "I'm so thankful not to miss this."

I have missed so much because of my distraction-prone brain and because of job pressures and travel. I am more motivated than ever to stay in tune with my remarkable wife and our precious kids. I do not want to miss my own life. So I give thanks and keep practicing.

THE FINE ART (AND RISK) OF ENGAGING

I do a little coaching with folks looking for love, alongside giving advice to married couples looking to recapture romance. I tell them, "Look, you won't get anywhere in love if you don't engage. Looking down and memorizing the tops of your shoes will not do it. You have to do whatever it takes to work through and get over fear, anxiety, pride, conceit to become a person who notices, acknowledges, and engages with others. You start relationships that way, and you build them every day by continuing to notice and connect with people."

Disengage, or never engage, and you miss the foundation of romantic love.

My son Solomon is, at this writing, nine years old, extremely bright, and very handsome. Recently we went on an evening bike ride together. On the return trip, we saw two little girls on the sidewalk with one very cute dog. Solomon loves dogs and seems to have a way with little girls (which I did not know until that evening ride). He kicked his bike into park, walked over to them, and asked if he could pet their dog. They smiled and nodded. As he knelt down to engage with the dog, he engaged with the girls, telling them how much he loved dogs and that this was one of the cutest ones he had ever seen.

Then my boy very casually and naturally asked the girls, "What are your names?" They happily responded, and Solomon followed up with another question. "What are your teachers' names?" The girls answered, and Solomon perked up, smiling broadly, and said, "Oh, so that's why I thought I knew you. I helped out in your class last week. I remember seeing you there when I was helping with math. Well, I guess I better go."

At this point, I couldn't help but notice that the two sidewalk sisters were beaming smiles in my boy's direction. I watched Solomon get back on his two-wheeler, unkick the stand, and start to ride off, but then he looked back and said to his sweet, responsive new friends, "Thanks for letting me pet your dog!"

What I realized that night, afresh, was that my nine-year-old son has the "it factor" when it comes to engaging with people. He followed his heart and took a risk to stop his bike when he saw something he liked (a cute dog), and he engaged. He asked permission to pet the dog (showing honor for the owners' boundaries) and then complimented the girls on what they obviously had in common with him (love of dogs). He then took a risk to learn their names and pointed out one more thing they had in common: a school connection. He expressed gratitude and said a polite goodbye. His ease at engaging others made his ol' dad swell with pride. Someday, when Solomon is more interested in girls than he is in dogs, these attributes are going to serve him well.

What I have just described, and what Solomon is already discovering, is something that psychologists are calling "attunement." In its simplest form, attunement means to be aware of, and responsive to, another. In romantic relationships, it also involves getting so in sync with your partner that the rest of the world falls away.

Monty Roberts, the world-famous Horse Whisperer, coined the term *join up* for the wordless communication that happens between a human and a horse, when a cowboy studies and learns to speak horse language. This language, as it turns out, is a precise series of gestures between equals (rather than master-slave control) that builds trust and affection. It is magical to watch this connection take place between the human and the animal kingdom. (Google "Monty Roberts" and "join up" for some examples on YouTube!) But it is even more incredible to experience an emotional join-up between a man and a woman.

In marriage, we join up or attune to each other by speaking each other's love language, both verbally and nonverbally. Not as a way to control or manipulate but as a way to experience oneness together, partnership, and to deeply communicate honor, interest, affection, and love.

This is a very good thing for increasing the passion factor in any relationship. Misty and I are now in the marriage-enhancing habit of pausing, focusing, and tuning in to each other at some point every day. Of course, most of the joy that comes more naturally for us now didn't just happen by accident. It's a hard-earned happiness, honed through mutual willingness, proactive effort, and lots of practice.

TOUCHY-FEELY PEOPLE

I tell singles in search of romantic love, "You must *touch* people." (Appropriately, of course.) And in this area of connecting, no country on earth excels like Italy.

It is no secret that Italians tend to be emotionally, verbally, and physically expressive souls. They cannot imagine a conversation without using their hands to gesture or touch each other when talking. Even Italian journalists can't keep their hands from flying as they report the news on TV. But you might be surprised at just how wide the difference is between the amount of touching that Anglo-Saxon countries experience and the amount experienced by Latin cultures.

In a famous study in the 1960s, people were observed in a cafe, talking for an hour, in several countries. In England, the land of the prim, private, and proper, there was no touching. Zilch. Americans weren't much better, touching an average of only twice an hour. In France, however, the touching shot up to 110 times an hour. In a later study, it was discovered that Italians touched each other almost three times more often during a typical conversation than did the average French couple! (Atsa lotta skin-to-skin connection.)[1]

What does casual touching have to do with passion in marriage? Study after study shows that couples who literally can't keep their hands off each other, even in old age, are more in tune with each other. Their hearts even tend to line up and beat in the same rhythm in their sleep. When people are under stress, scientists note, anxiety starts to diminish when a lover holds them or grasps their hand.[2]

It is not surprising, then, that couples who hold hands in public or easily reach to stroke each other's cheek or pat a shoulder are the ones most likely to get lucky back at the ol' villa. Small, regular, tender touches form the threads of connection between men and women that eventually create long-lasting bonds of passion, commitment, and romance.

In my advice on dating, I tell women, "Casually, in conversation, form a bridge of connection by touching the top of a man's hand or his shoulder or arm." Just a slight touch says, without words, "I'm not afraid. I'm not a prude or uptight. I am comfortable." It is incredible what that little touch does to draw a man to a woman and dispel misperceptions of who she is and the need to protect himself.

I advise men, "Just gently touch your date's back as you escort her through a crowd or a door. Don't put your hand too low or too high or leave it there long. Just a respectful touch." And that slight touch of gallant manhood is often the cue for her to drop her unease and comfortably make a connection.

Anyone who has fallen in love can point to the moment when their eyes met someone else's in more than a casual glance. It is the look in the eyes that often takes a relationship from polite attention to real engagement, especially if followed up with comments and questions that go below the surface. If you accompany this conversation with appropriate casual, slight touches, it can seal a significant connection deep in the brain's memory files. When you apply the secrets of deep engagement, whether you are on a first date with someone new or the hundredth date with your spouse, you'll find that the person you're with will naturally open their heart and communicate more vulnerably and deeply with you.

THE SECRETS OF ATTUNEMENT: FROM ITALIAN MEN

When it comes to joining up to their lovers via talking and touching, gazing and questioning, sharing and affirming, Italians really have it going *on*. Let's unlock some of the other secrets to engaging deeply with the opposite sex.

He is generous with compliments and expressions of gratitude. An Italian man will "work hard to improve himself and to let the object of his affection know that she is the one. When an Italian man meets a woman for the first time, he discovers her greatest attribute—her smile or her generosity or her long legs—and applauds it as though he was the first to do so. He makes a woman feel as though she is special and full of potential just in the way he looks at her. The reflection she will see of herself in his eyes will leave her full of desire and breathless with anticipation. An Italian man always gets the girl because he makes her fall in love with him as much as he makes her fall in love with herself. That's the secret!"[3]

Of course, the Italian man does not always get the girl, but his way with a woman increases the odds greatly. And one of his most powerful ways of creating positive connection is through showing appreciation and gratitude. Who doesn't like to be thanked? It is a simple but profound—and paradoxical—truth: if you want to be appreciated, the most effective way to make that happen is simply to say thank you. One of the things I've noticed about the happiest, healthiest married couples is that they "live in gratitude" with each other. Make it a habit to thank your mate for the dozens of things they do that make your life easier. "Thank you, babe, for cooking that delicious supper." "I so appreciate you washing my car today!" "I love the way you are so sweet to pitch in with the kids' bedtime even though I know you are exhausted too." Notice the gifts in your spouse; acknowledge and verbally appreciate them. Shower the woman you love with sincere compliments, express your gratitude for all she does, and watch her blossom like a flower in sunshine.

He sets up conditions for meaningful conversation. Italian men know, perhaps better than men from any other country, that the way to a woman's heart is often through her brain, through meaningful conversation. According to the Italian website Zoomata, in a recent magazine survey of more than one thousand Italian men, 68 percent reported carrying a book to the beach to encourage conversation with women. About 80 percent of those men toted the Bible or Dante's *Divine Comedy*—not what Americans would consider a good beach read, but Italian guys obviously know something about connecting to women on a deep level and are unafraid to go there.[4]

Books on the beach seem to do it for Italians. But here in America, I have noticed that nothing sets up conversation like a bark in the park. Having a dog with you increases the likelihood of conversation by 2,456 percent, according to one informal survey I made up in my own head. Unless your dog is a Doberman or a pit bull. If you want to meet people, get a dog with big, adorable eyes and soft fur. A kitten or a bunny or even a lemur could also work. It just needs to be an animal that looks soft to the touch and begs to be held.

He uses the art of tender touch. Finally, Italian men are masters at those casual, zinger touches that make a woman's knees go weak. "Italian men worship the female form and pay attention to details—from sweetly caressing your cheek in a passionate moment to playfully twisting your hair on the beach."[5]

The growing research on the value of touch to our well-being and feelings of connection, bonding, and intimacy is astounding. Neuroscientists have found that physical touch activates the area of the brain that links to feelings of reward and compassion. A simple touch can trigger the release of oxytocin (the "love hormone") and also stimulate the vagus nerve, which evokes feelings of compassion. Gentle touches not only soothe us; they are healthy for us, calming cardiovascular stress and strengthening the immune system. All these emotions bond us and make us feel we're on the same team, working toward a common goal. In fact, NBA teams whose players touch each other more—in pats on the back and manly guy hugs—win more games!

> To touch can be to give life.
>
> —MICHELANGELO

A gentle brush of a woman's arm can boost a man's chances in love: one research study showed that two-thirds of women agreed to dance with a man who touched her on the arm a second or two before making the request.[6] Never underestimate the power of even a small, glancing touch to increase the bond in your marriage.

THE SECRETS OF ATTUNEMENT:
FROM ITALIAN WOMEN

Lest you think that Italian men have the corner on ways to successfully engage with the opposite sex, I'd like you to meet a few Italian women who have much to teach American ladies about passionate love.

She never doubts her feminine power. "My Zia [Aunt] Concettina is built of peasant stock—a rotund but firm belly, broad shoulders and strong-like-bull legs—but she will always be the picture of femininity to me. In a typical day, she might carry a 30-pound grandbaby on her hip, wash the floor on her knees, and lift bushels of tomatoes over her head. But everywhere we go, men (and even women) flock to her like Tony Soprano to prosciutto. I think the twinkle in her eye, her contagious laugh and bawdy humor do the trick. She is unafraid to swing her hips and make eyes at complete strangers, especially men."[7]

She sees her face and body as an artist's canvas. Journalist Hugo McCafferty is an Irishman married for ten years to an Italian woman, and now the proud father of three Irish-Italian children. In an email interview, Hugo shared this insight about Italian women: "Italian women don't just throw something on, and from young girls to doddering nonnas there's a coherence in what they wear, a look. And it gives them confidence; even the very plain or average looking Italian woman moves with a certain confidence, and that is in itself very attractive. Even the non-lookers are, from a distance, lookers; the beautiful ones are off the scale." It seems that Italian women know they are fearfully and wonderfully made by God, but they are not afraid to adorn God's handiwork with some tasteful artistic draping.

> At the dressing table, every woman has a chance to be an artist, and art, as Aristotle said, "completes what nature left unfinished."
>
> —SOPHIA LOREN

She is openly passionate. Italian women feel things deeply and are known to wear their emotions on their sleeves. "Whether welling up in tears listening to Celine Dion, or rapturously throwing their arms around you for no good reason, there's never a dull moment," McCaffery wrote.

She is also open with her feelings of gratitude and admiration for her man. I am the grateful recipient of sincere compliments from my wife that draw me to her and have a bit of healing ointment in them. I grew up with two older brothers who were anything but encouraging, and I felt inadequate from a young age. This left what therapists call a core wound in my vulnerable, little-boy heart. Any betrayal, abandonment, or feelings of failure would reopen that wound. I had hoped that success would silence the long-ago voices of shame. But having a *New York Times* bestseller did not fix it. Entrepreneur of the Year didn't do it, and being inducted into the Speaker Hall of Fame didn't cure me. No achievement soothed the inner pain of inadequacy.

Then one day Misty shared with me that she was talking with a friend of hers who wanted to publish a book. She told her friend in response to a request for guidance, "Well, Steve knows everything about it. He would be so happy to help in any way. He has so much experience and truly loves helping new authors find their way. He also loves getting good, helpful resources out to as many people as possible. Let me talk to him."

Whoo Hoo! came a shout from an aching and inadequate soul. In truth, the shout felt as if it came from a ten-year-old boy. Misty could not have said anything better to help me feel more competent as a man. The effect of her sincere, uplifting belief in me was, as we say in the psych world, reparative. My wife's confidence in my abilities and character made me walk a little taller, and the old wound inside me started to heal.

The point I'm trying to make to women reading this book is that you have so much power in the words you use, to both build up your man's self-esteem and heal old hurts left by others in his past. See if you can figure out where your husband may have been hurt the most as a child, and compliment him, sincerely, when you see he needs encouragement. And if you speak highly of your man in front of others as well, this is a double blessing. No matter how self-assured your husband may appear, most of us men are really just little boys inside, hanging by our knees on the monkey bars, hoping our girl will notice and tell us how strong and talented we are.

There really can't be too many compliments from husband to wife, or wife to husband, in a marriage. Almost all of us, men and women, have endured plenty of criticism, and we hear it over and over in our minds. A marriage can be a great healing force for these old wounds, applying the balm of affirmation.

She is, by nature, a foodie. Italian women grow up knowing their way around a garden and a kitchen. They savor freshly prepared, beautiful, healthy food, with none of the food phobias so common to American women.

"They love food, they live for food, they eat it, they talk about it, they clap their hands together with excitement when they see a restaurant menu."[8] In other words, Italian women seem to instinctively know that food is a way to connection, to sensual experiences, to love! (More on the connection between love and food in chapter 4.)

She has a disarming sense of humor. Not only are Italian women witty, but they are also more than willing to laugh at themselves. "Any man will tell you, there's nothing sexier than a feisty sense of humor, and Italian women have that in spades," one blogger wrote. Sharing humor is a great way to become quickly attuned to your partner.[9] As the beloved and funny Danish pianist Victor Borge once said, "The closest distance between two people is a laugh."

She knows that beauty is more about self-esteem than physical attributes. Sophia Loren, still sizzling at eighty, wrote this important piece of advice to women: "You must all, somewhere deep in your hearts, believe that you have a special beauty that is like no other and that is so valuable that you must not abandon it. Indeed, you must learn to cherish it." She also said, "Nothing makes a woman more beautiful than the belief that she is beautiful." We've all met women who would not necessarily have won any beauty contests but who had a certain something that others found irresistible. The word for that certain something, I think, is *allure*, which means "the quality of being powerfully or mysteriously attractive or fascinating." The good news is that a woman can be alluring without being a cover model. (Case in point: the previously mentioned Aunt Concettina.) A woman with inner confidence who believes she is beautiful, feminine, sexy, fun, and smart can be alluring to her husband (and everyone else) all her life. One way to be alluring is to be fully aware of the man who sits across the breakfast table from you, focus on his best qualities, and tease them out of him one by one, as only an expertly engaging woman can.

ALL THE TIME IN THE WORLD FOR YOU, MY LOVE

Though expats from America and other time-sensitive cultures may not consider it a positive value, Italians and people of many other Mediterranean countries have an almost blatant disregard for the clock. They rarely seem in a hurry and are typically open and welcoming to drop-in visitors. Contrast that to Americans with precious little margin in their fast-paced lives, who feel not joy but irritation at a friend dropping by unannounced, and think only of what is not getting crossed off on the ever-pressing to-do list. Westerners make lots of lists; Mediterraneans linger and make love.

Imagine a whole country enjoying a built-in, guilt-free, daily naptime! Italians say that the only people who are awake during the midafternoon siesta are "foreigners and fools." This appreciation of rest, this lack of hurriedness, feels pretty wonderful when couples are completely focused on each other, asking questions, touching, leaning back to listen, admiring, pouring another glass of wine on a late summer's eve. (Perhaps they have more stamina for paying rapt attention to each other because everyone just had a long, refreshing nap.) Their attitude and body language convey to each other, "You matter. I'm fully present and enjoying every single aspect of being with you, delightful person that you are!" Who wouldn't swoon over that sort of attention? Who wouldn't feel cherished, valued, loved?

Attunement is, in short, all about paying closer attention to each other. It is getting our mind off the dozens of things that pull at our attention; it's tending fully to the love of our life for a few moments a day, every day. We can do this through our eyes, our body language, the way we prioritize unhurried time with each other, the way we affirm, compliment, and build up our partner in ways that make them happy to be a man, delighted to be a woman. (If you don't know what words of praise and honor make them happy, ask!) It is also about paying closer attention to ourselves and feeding our senses, allowing passion to rise and flow naturally, appreciating our inner selves and presenting ourselves in ways that make us feel unique, classy, fun, sexy. It is about being fully present for your lover in proactive, sense-drenched ways on a regular basis.

A beautiful thing happens when we start paying attention to each other. It is by participating more in your relationship that you breathe life into it.

—STEVE MARABOLI, *UNAPOLOGETICALLY YOU*

Thirteen Ways to Keep Your Lover Attuned

1. Be aware of the art of subtle touch. Men, try putting your hand on the small of your wife's back when guiding her through a door, or put your hand over her hand while driving, or tenderly bring her hand to your lips and kiss it. Reach across the table and caress her cheek with your hand. Women, gently rub the back of your man's neck while he is driving, or lay your head on his shoulder while watching TV. Put your arm in the crook of his when walking. Give him a love pat as you scoot around him in the kitchen to reach for a glass, letting your body gently graze his in passing. (As the title of one book states, sex begins in the kitchen. Perhaps it's because there are all kinds of opportunities to bump into each other there.)

2. Meet at a coffee shop or cafe in the middle of the day, or get together for a glass of wine after work and pretend to be two people deeply attracted to each other, meeting up for a first date. Flirt, steal a kiss, gaze, laugh. Touch, touch, touch—like Italians do!

3. Give compliments that affirm each other's masculinity or femininity. Wives, say something that helps your man feel like a man! ("I love the way you took charge of that meeting the other day." "Look at how easily you moved all those boxes upstairs! I sometimes forget how strong you are!" "You are a wonderful lover. That was amazing.") Men, help your lady feel glad she is a woman! ("Your beauty, when you're just standing near the window in the sunlight, takes my breath away." "I love how tender you are with our kids." "Knowing that your smile and your arms are waiting for me at the end of the day keeps me

going.") Don't hesitate to simply ask each other, "What words of affirmation from me make you feel happy to be my husband? Glad to be my wife?"

4. Create some extra margin in your life for lingering. (If at all possible, keep a portion of your weekends free to allow for at least a half day of unscheduled time together.) Have a regular happy hour (or half hour if time is short) after work sitting together on the porch in summer or cuddling up on a couch or soaking in a bubble bath. Enjoy a few minutes of pillow talk before sleep. You can share a relaxing beverage, unwind, and share your day. (Be sure to ask questions as well as share your thoughts.) Some couples' schedules allow for coffee chats in the morning (especially on weekends), and they love to begin their days with a bit of lingering and connection.

5. Give some extra thought to what you are wearing. Colors, cut, and other elements of style can make all of us feel a little bit sexier. Women, bring out your inner Italian and show a bit more shoulder or cleavage or leg, or wear something form fitting when you are alone with your man. Wear pretty lingerie under your clothes to remind yourself that you are a sensual woman. Men, up your game a bit in the wardrobe department. Maybe it's time to lose those old faded, baggy jeans and get some new jeans that fit and flatter your assets. Exchange your "Git 'er Dun" T-shirt for some classier, slogan-free shirts that are still comfortable. (Black knit shirts with any kind of collar look great on most men. Throw on a jacket, and look out, Lola.) Ladies, ask your husband what kinds of clothes and colors he likes best on you, and try to honor his preferences when you can (within reason). Men, notice or ask what your wife loves to see you wear. Wear clothes in colors that set off your best features.

Even comfy bum-around-the-house clothes can be sexy if you put a little thought into them.

6. Women, ponder Sophia Loren's advice to "believe that you have a special beauty that is like no other," and never abandon this part of you; cherish your inner beauty. For "nothing makes a woman more beautiful than the belief that she is beautiful." Do you truly believe that you are beautiful? If not, search deep inside and find the beauty God sees in you. Begin to treat yourself as if you were uniquely beautiful, as if there were no other woman on earth like you. The confidence that emanates from a woman who cherishes the beauty God placed inside her will prove irresistible. Whether or not you realize it, how you feel about and treat yourself is often how you teach others to feel about and treat you.

7. Men, you may not want to bring a copy of the Bible or Dante's *Divine Comedy* to the beach, but try listening to or reading a book that inspires you or teaches you something new, that goes a little deeper and causes you to ask yourself new questions. When the time is right and you and your lady are lingering together—on a walk or sitting out on the porch before dinner—share some of the thoughts you are reading, ask her opinion, and listen to her response. Show that you value her insight and perspective.

8. Laugh together whenever possible. Laughter is one of the world's most underrated aphrodisiacs. Watch funny movies or cartoons or share a hilarious YouTube video that you know your lover will enjoy. Never be afraid to tell a good story on yourself, as sharing our flaws with humor is a powerful way of connecting with our soul mate. Not long ago, our family sat around the table laughing our heads off as each member recounted some hilarious moment they remembered. Misty recalled a night

when we were watching a weather report in the midst of a blizzard. A local weatherman was out in the snow, reporting. He was wearing a hoodie over what appeared to be several stocking caps. But in order to hear, he had his ears sticking out of the overstuffed hoodie. The top of the hoodie formed a fine point, like a steeple. It looked more like a spacesuit than a weatherman's jacket. So I adopted a voice like ET and spoke over him. "This is Mark the Martian reporting live from a blizzard here on planet Earth." Misty laughed for two days after that. (I stopped laughing after a day and a half.) We relived it all over again months later, and it seemed just as funny; our sides were aching. Try going back in time to things that once tickled your funny bone as a couple, and bring them up at dinner tonight. The laughter will do you good!

9. Don't be afraid to be passionate about preparing and serving delicious food! Instead of thinking like a glutton—piling up a plate at the local all-you-can-eat buffet—think like a food connoisseur, pausing to notice and savor the flavors of a fresh, ripe peach or a perfectly cooked salmon. There was a cooking show (recently cancelled) called *The Taste*, about creating one perfect bite. The contestants had to serve the judges one ideal spoonful of their culinary creation. So much thought went into such a tiny amount of food! Food scientists tell us that we get the most taste from our food in the first three bites, so try slowing down the process of eating together and truly enjoying the first few bites of a fabulous meal. If you do this, you will find yourself both satisfied and full with smaller portions. Focus on quality of taste and freshness in what you eat, rather than on quantity, and you'll discover that food can become a shared passion and delight that also contributes to your health and happiness. (More on this later.)

10. Make saying thank you a part of your daily habits, and you will be amazed at how these two small words, given generously, strengthen the bond of love and romance. Try this: every evening, between dinner and lights-out, when you are together, thank the one you love for at least one thing they did or one thing they are that blesses your life. And if you kept a list of those things mentioned, it would make a wonderful gift on an anniversary or birthday. It would also serve as a reminder to you, when you go through a rough spot, of all the things you are grateful for, beneath whatever the current conflict might be.

11. Remember, the eyes are the window to your passionate soul. Don't be afraid to gaze at your mate; let your eyes linger over his or her face and form. Search for your partner's eyes across a crowded room, and give a wink, a knowing glance, or a shy, sexy smile. See how much you can say to each other without saying a word. It can be incredibly erotic. If you watch any romantic movie with an Italian man or woman as the lead, you will observe how they so expertly and naturally use their eyes to charm the opposite sex—via longing gazes, flirtatious glances, raised eyebrows, winks, or knowing looks. There is a reason why Italian men are known for having bedroom eyes, and it isn't all about their eyes' shape or color. It is because an Italian man knows how to convey desire for a woman, take her under his spell with a look, whether or not she can understand a word of the language he is speaking.

12. Try being more open with your emotions, especially the positive or tender ones. If you feel a surge of gratitude for the beauty of the day, or the love of your wife, or the cuteness of your kids, don't keep it to yourself. Say it. Say it with energy and passion. People are drawn to those who love and appreciate the small

things in life, who don't shy away from expressing their joy or sharing how a song touches their emotions or conveying how much compassion they feel for someone's pain.

13. Practice getting in sync with your spouse regularly. It requires a certain letting go of the day, quieting the noise in your own head to link up with what your mate is feeling or thinking. Pretend you are a therapist (or "marriage whisperer"), and notice not only what your husband or wife is saying but also their body language, their tone of voice. Respond thoughtfully rather than reacting impulsively. When they volunteer a thought or information, follow up by asking a question about what they just shared. Don't move on too quickly to your own agenda. Listening deeply and paying full attention to your lover as they talk is one of the greatest gifts you can give them.

Poet John Fox said it beautifully:

> When someone deeply listens to you
> it is like holding out a dented cup
> you've had since childhood
> and watching it fill up with
> cold, fresh water.
> When it balances on top of the brim,
> you are understood.
> When it overflows and touches your skin,
> you are loved . . ."[10]

CHAPTER 3

THE SECRET OF PLAYFULNESS

The main preoccupation of the Spanish is having a good time and they have a zest for life matched by few other peoples. They take childish pleasure in making the most of everything and grasp every opportunity to make merry.

—DAVID HAMPSHIRE, *LIVING AND WORKING IN SPAIN*

You can learn more about a person in an hour of play than in a lifetime of conversation.

—PLATO

If there were a nation that could be dubbed Most Passionately Playful People on Earth, surely the Spanish would be it. Spaniards are well known for their unbridled enthusiasm for soccer (or "futbol"), but given half a chance, they can turn anything into a contest, game, or party.

Case in point:

On the last Wednesday of every August, the small town of Bunol, Spain, swells with thousands of lucky ticketholders from all over the world. Around eleven o'clock in the morning, truckloads of ripe tomatoes (more than 120,000 pounds) arrive in the city streets. Then one brave soul starts climbing to the top of a two-story-tall greased wooden pole. If successful, he touches a ham ensconced at the top of the pole, then throws a hefty slice of the cured pork down to the street below. (As one does.) This, of course, starts the firing of water cannons, which signals the start of (wait for it) the world's biggest food fight.

For one hour, thousands of partygoers throw and mash tomatoes into each other's faces, hair, and clothes in a chaotic frenzy of "fun." It's a wild tomato pasting, with every man for himself. Actually, it is every man and woman for themselves, and the event allows for a lot of touching, squishing, falling down together in a heap of laughter, marinara, and mock fighting. Messy but sensual play for the uninhibited (or desperately bored).

After an hour, when the streets are running red with the blood of ripe tomatoes, and the acid of the fruit is performing a citywide skin peel, there is another firing of water cannons and, just as suddenly as the festival began, the party is over. Fire trucks move in to spray down the streets, while people head to the local river to wash themselves off.

This annual affair is called La Tomatina and has been going on since 1945. Prior to 2013, up to fifty thousand people crammed into the city for this event, but it got too crazy, even for Spaniards, and thereafter it has become a coveted ticketed affair.

"Possible theories on how the Tomatina began include a local food fight among friends, a juvenile class war, a volley of tomatoes from bystanders at a carnival parade. . . . One popular theory is that disgruntled townspeople attacked city councilmen with tomatoes during a town celebration. Whatever happened to begin the tradition, it was enjoyed so much that it was repeated the next year, and the year after that, and so on."[1]

There is no political or religious or romantic meaning to the mass tomato hurling. In other words, for seventy years the people of Spain have thrown tomatoes at each other for no logical reason. Somebody just thought it sounded like fun, and tens of thousands of fun-seeking Spaniards soon agreed.

And here I rest my case. Spaniards just wanna have fun.

Before we look into what we might learn from the people of Spain about adopting a more playful spirit, let's begin with another question. What does playfulness have to do with passion and romance?

Glad you asked.

PLAYFULNESS AND ATTRACTION

If you want to remain attractive to, and attract, the opposite sex, you may want to consider upping your fun-to-be-around factor.

In one study, women ranked the following traits (out of sixteen possible ones) as most important to them in a long-term mate.[2]

1. kindness and understanding
2. sense of humor
3. fun loving
4. playful

Note that three out of four of the top traits that a woman wants in a man fall under the umbrella of playfulness.

Men placed similar importance on playful personalities in women. In fact, the trait men valued most in a woman was a sense of humor. A fun-loving nature was third, playfulness fifth. It may surprise the ladies to know that physical attractiveness came in at a low spot of number nine in the list of traits men said they most looked for in a long-term romantic partner.[3]

Researchers speculated that "a woman's playfulness ... may signal her youth and fertility." I don't know about that, but I do know that men love being around women who are positive, playful, and fun.[4]

From my casual observation of married couples over the years, I have to say that spouses who are generally upbeat, enthusiastic, and game for a new adventure together or can be quickly distracted into having some spontaneous fun and are easy laughers tend also to have passionate marriages.

Before I even saw Misty for the first time, it was her laugh that drew me to her. I heard this joyful laughter in the middle of a crowd of people, and it sounded, to me at the time, something like hope. I was going through one of the darkest periods of my life back then and felt compelled to follow the laughter to its source. And, oh man, what a source it turned out to be! But I'm ahead of myself. Let me back up and set the scene.

Every year, NewLife Ministries plans a fun trip that we offer to our radio listeners and supporters. Over a decade ago, my team and I were brainstorming ideas for the trip, when I suggested, "Why don't we do a land cruise?"

"You mean, like a fake cruise?" my team asked.

"Yes!" I said with the kind of enthusiasm my staff has come to know means their lives are about to get interesting.

So NewLife booked a lovely hotel in Dana Point, California. Since we were landlocked, we hauled in truckloads of sand to spread over the lawn, then stationed fire pits here and there, where people could gather and visit. Going with the cruise theme, we had lots of buffets, even some at midnight. We provided plenty of "onboard entertainment." The original host of TV's *The Newlywed Game*, Bob Eubanks, drove down from Hollywood to emcee a special version of the classic game show, recruiting several couples from among our attendees as contestants. Long-married pop singers Billy Davis Jr. and Marilyn McCoo gave us a stellar performance one night. Then John Townsend and his band provided the music for the last evening, "NewLife Dance Night," and it was anything but square.

The dance was held on the fake beach, and I was visiting with a few folks around a fire pit when I heard the aforementioned joyful laughter in the distance. Following the sound, I made my way over to a cluster of people who were obviously having a good time. It was then I first spied the owner of that infectious laugh. They were calling her Misty, and she had the face of an angel. Like, seriously. Find a picture of a beautiful

Christmas angel, with fair blonde hair and beautiful blue eyes and a heavenly smile, and you've got Misty. I mumbled hello and had to use some real effort not to linger. But I forced myself to keep moving on, mingling with the crowd as I felt a good host should.

It was more than a year before I saw or talked to Misty again, but suffice it to say, I never forgot the melodious laughter of this mystery woman or the gleaming smile on her face. I could never have dreamed then, when I was going through so much private agony, that one day this sweet, funny, beautiful lady would become my wife.

Many years later, Misty's playful spirit, joyful heart, and easy laughter continue to light up my life. A playful sense of humor is not only what first attracted me to Misty; it is still a key ingredient in the emotional super glue that keeps us bonded. Why, just the other day, Misty and I were out to lunch together at a cafe. She was irritated with me that day, for a reason I can't remember now. As chance would have it, I said something funny at just the right moment. She did not want to laugh. She was angry with me and wanted to stay angry. But my comment was funny, very funny, and the laughter started to squeak out of her. She turned her head away from me, shielded her eyes and mouth, losing the battle against humor. She bent over, trying with all her might not to let out that laughter. But she failed, and failed miserably. She cried, she laughed so hard. People were staring, she laughed so hard. And I reveled in my victory! Truly it was our victory, because laughter and play had won over resentments and cold shoulders.

If you've read many books on marriage in the last three decades, you've probably heard of Dr. John Gottman. He is a marriage therapist famous for his "love lab," where he spent years researching what makes some marriages last for a lifetime and what contributes to the massive failure of others. In time, he was able to predict with an amazing amount of accuracy which couples would stay together and which would eventually divorce. One of his significant findings was that couples who are playful have a better chance of remaining together. He found that a general habit of playfulness between partners—even in times of tension—helped soothe the inevitable hurts and mis-attunements that pop up in marriage.

In other words, prioritizing playfulness in your relationship is serious business if you want to enjoy passion for a lifetime.

PLAYFULNESS AND SEX

For sheer vitality and passion for life the Spanish have few equals, and whatever Spain can be accused of it's never dull or boring.[5]

—DAVID HAMPSHIRE, *LIVING AND WORKING IN SPAIN*

Passion has been in my DNA for generations.

—JULIO IGLESIAS

Throwing tomatoes at each other for an hour may not be your cup of tea (or pot of pasta). Still, we can glean from our Spanish friends plenty of practical insights into how to put more play into our every day. Another positive stat about Spaniards is that—beyond being playful—they consistently show up as the most sexually happy folks in the world.

In a recent study of nearly ten thousand men and women from Spain, a whopping 90 percent said they were sexually satisfied. (And this satisfaction rose over time with a stable relationship as opposed to casual encounters, which is an encouraging statistic for those of us who value both passion and long-term commitment.) In contrast, only 48 percent of Americans report being sexually satisfied.[6] This is a huge discrepancy, somewhat depressing for the American team. And not only do Spaniards find sex satisfying; they are also often cited in international surveys as being the world's best lovers. In other words, they seem to be masterful at both receiving and giving sexual love.

Love Stats

THE WORLD'S BEST AND WORST LOVERS

Personal Note from Steve: It is not my observation that Germans are smelly or Turks are sweaty. I'm just reporting the conclusions of the researchers who put together this list.

WORLD'S WORST LOVERS	WORLD'S BEST LOVERS
1. Germany (too smelly)	1. Spain
2. England (too lazy)	2. Brazil
3. Sweden (too quick)	3. Italy
4. Holland (too dominating)	4. France
5. America (too rough)	5. Ireland
6. Greece (too lovey-dovey)	6. South Africa
7. Wales (too selfish)	7. Australia
8. Scotland (too loud)	8. New Zealand
9. Turkey (too sweaty)	9. Denmark
10. Russia (too hairy)	10. Canada

"German Men Are World's Worst Lovers . . .," September 2009, *The Telegraph*: www.telegraph.co.uk/news/newstopics/howaboutthat/6241440/German-men-are -worlds-worst-lovers-with-English-men-in-second-place.html.

I don't know about you, but I can't help but wonder, "What's the deal here? Why are Spaniards enjoying significantly happier sex lives than the rest of the world?"

I don't think it is a coincidence that a country that boasts such high sexual satisfaction is also known as the most playful country in the world. A playful attitude and enjoyment of sex go together like peas and carrots. This isn't just true for the modern world; it has been so for centuries.

In the Old Testament, there is an interesting phrase about Isaac, who was found "sporting with Rebekah his wife" (Gen. 26:8 KJV). In the context of this story from the book of Genesis, it is clear that this married couple wasn't playing badminton or Parcheesi.

I rather like the word *sporting* as a euphemism for sexual relations between husband and wife. For as I've hinted, and as sex therapists will agree, there is an undeniable connection between playfulness and the relaxed and passionate joy of sex. The more relaxed and playful we can be with our mates, the more fun and natural our intimate lives will be.

I wish I could tell you that I bounded into marriage with Misty as the fully formed husband of her dreams—a confident, playful, sexy Casanova.

The reality was that I had a lot to learn about *joie de vivre* in the ol' marital boudoir. Thankfully, my new bride not only had a heart for joyful fun but also had a spirit of perseverance when it came to making our sex life all it could be.

We did not have sex before we were married, so both of us had high hopes for the honeymoon. If my memory is correct, I might have made a few boastful claims about how great that experience would prove to be for her. That might have been one of the dumbest things I've ever said, because the intimacy on our honeymoon was a long way from the sexy fireworks I'd promised Misty.

Let's just say I did not know what I did not know.

A few months into our marriage, Misty casually asked me to take a look at a website of a health spa in Arizona where a pair of married physicians would be conducting a workshop on sexual intimacy. It was designed for people who were not experiencing fulfillment in this area of their marriage. I took a glance at the website and responded, "Oh, how nice and helpful."

Then I looked at Misty's raised eyebrows. My response quickly morphed into, "Ohhhhh, I get it," accompanied by a hangdog expression on my face.

A willing spirit—in place of our pride—is all we need sometimes to change the course of our lives for the better. I called upon God to grant me an extra dose of it, and he provided. So to help me learn what I didn't know that I didn't know, we went to Arizona for five days and four nights.

I was careful to make sure that this sex camp, as I started jokingly calling it, was going to be led in a professional way and not organized by wild, kinky sex gurus in flowing robes, smelling of incense and impropriety. Everything checked out well. The first evening, however, was predictably uncomfortable. In the mix of about fifty participants were many who looked like the walking dead. We were each asked to share why we were there, and several couples admitted that the thrill was gone, the passion had passed, and for some the marriage was on life support.

Over the following days, Misty and I absorbed so much information that it changed how we related to each other both inside and outside the bedroom. If I had to sum up what we learned about how to make our sex life more fulfilling, I would say this: they taught us to remove the pressure and seriousness that can so subtly sabotage lovemaking and to relax, have fun, enjoy each other more. In other words, make sex more playful! It was especially fun to watch the transformation of the couples around us as the seminar progressed: wrinkled brows and tight lips relaxed into youthful smiles and laughter. The walking dead came alive as passion returned to their relationship. In just a handful of days, everyone there (except one holdout from England who refused to talk at all) began to journey from serious despair into the realm of playful joy. Lots of what we gleaned at the workshop is woven through the passion secrets presented in this book. Turns out that passion is less about sexual technique than about the joy in the journey, and about discovering intimacy with the whole person we married—soul, emotions, mind, and body.

Misty and I emerged from the desert of Arizona a different couple. We were not instantly better at anything, but we had insight into our problem, a path and a plan to make our marriage more about playful, sexy closeness than about an anxiety-producing, performance-based duty. When I look at who we were as a couple ten years ago and who we are today, there's such a difference! Our intimacy is now full of excitement, playfulness, and even laughter at times. Good laughter. The kind that nurtures. With all our defects and deficiencies, we are becoming the couple we've always wanted to be. No longer bound by fear or a lack of wisdom. Free to experience what God has for all of us. We want that for you.

CULTIVATING YOUR OWN "ROMANCE" LANGUAGE

For women the best aphrodisiacs are words. The G-spot
is in the ears. He who looks for it below there is wasting
his time.[7]

—ISABEL ALLENDE

A recent headline in the *Daily Mail* boasted, "Spain's the Place to Live! Spanish Is the Happiest Language in the World—And Its People Are the Most in Love." The reason for this conclusion? Spanish users send the most love-related stickers on Viber, a free communication network. (This was ahead of the romantic countries of France, Italy, and Brazil.)[8] And in another study, scientists found that Spanish is the most positive language, using words like *love* and *laughter* more than does the language of any other major region in the world.

Not only does the Spanish language make liberal use of words associated with happiness, fun, and love, but also the sounds of its words, and even Spanish accents, are undeniably romantic. I mean, whose voice melted the hearts of women in the famous duet "To All the Girls I've Loved Before"? Was it the reedy-twang of country singer Willy Nelson that made women swoon? Or was it the silken, warm, melted-chocolate, Spanish-accented voice of Julio Iglesias that made females go weak in the knees?

Recently a friend told me, "Even though I don't speak fluent Spanish, I love speaking words of affection to my husband in Spanish. I will tell him, '*Te amo, te quiero, te adoro,*' which means, 'I love you, I want you,

I adore you.' But terms of endearment sound so much more sensual in another language."

You don't have to learn to speak fluent Spanish or Italian or French to take advantage of the romance of these languages. (Though learning a foreign language together could be a lot of fun and good for your marriage. More about that in a later chapter.) Just learn a few beautiful, romantic words or phrases in a Mediterranean language, then say them to your mate or pop them into a flirty text or email.

"I took my wife to France," said one of my good buddies. "And when I asked if she wanted to go see *l'Arc de Triomphe*—using my best French accent—she looked at me as though I had just turned into Maurice Chevalier. Suddenly she wasn't as interested in sightseeing in Paris as she was in hearing me pronounce more French phrases. Sometimes, even now, she will say, 'Speak some French to me, baby.' Don't ask me why, but she finds it sexy. Hey, I'll say 'cordon bleu' and sing 'Frere Jaques' all day if it puts her in that kind of mood!"

Another idea you can try to increase passion and playfulness, in plain old English, is to make your default vocabulary—especially around your mate—filled with words that are cheerful, optimistic, encouraging, loving, and flirty. Need some ideas to get you started?

Here are five phrases Misty tells me she loves hearing me say to her that make her feel loved and cherished, happy, and warm inside.

1. *"Where did you come from?"* This is my way of telling Misty that she is amazing, that I have no idea how she came up with some genius idea or thought she just shared. She knows it's my way of saying that her insight blows me away so much that she must have come from another solar system! But whenever I ask her this question, my Indiana-born girl just adorably answers, "Muncie."

2. *"Will you marry me?"* In a moment when I am suddenly overcome with appreciation of her, this question just naturally flows out of me. It's also a way to tell her that I would marry her again on the spot if I had just met her today.

3. *"I'd die for you."* This sentence pops out when I am in maximum love overload. I don't know any other way to tell her how I feel. I'm at a loss for words to say all that is in my heart for Misty. I am not at the level of saying I would walk on shards of glass for her, because that would really hurt, but death, well, I would do it in a heartbeat.

4. *"Could I put some nice lotion on your feet?"* She always playfully replies, "Yes, nice lotion, not mean lotion, please."

5. *"If all I ever got to experience of you was your collar bone, it would be enough."* No explanation needed.

Here are five phrases Misty says to me that strengthen my love for her and my desire to stop everything and pursue her in every way possible.

1. *"You know everything."* Obviously, I must admit I don't know everything. (Though I'd love to believe I do at times.) But what Misty is communicating to my sometimes insecure man-soul is that she believes in me. She believes I know a lot about a few things that matter and are of real significance to me.

2. *"You are my hero."* Misty is a strong and capable woman. But there are moments when she has needed me to show a certain kind of strength that she can lean into, and when—in these instances—she has called me her hero, well, nothing thrills me more. Every man has a boy inside him who longs to be a hero. I love it when I can be there for my wife, with all I have to give, in a moment when she needs my support.

3. *"You own me."* Misty may say this to me in a moment when I walk in and do or say something romantic that sweeps her off her feet, or she may say it when she walks in on me holding our little girl in my arms, singing to her gently. Another way she communicates that I alone hold her heart is by saying, "There's not another person on this planet I would rather live my life with." This is Misty's romantic equivalent of me telling her that I'd die for her. She usually says these things in a moment of

contentment, when she's aware that her heart is most at home with me, above anyone else.

4. *"You smell so good, I can't stand it."* I was at an airport, my flight delayed, time to kill, when I stumbled upon and purchased a man's cologne made by Brook's Brothers. I'd soon discover that this fragrance holds almost supernatural power over my wife. When I wear it, Misty clings to me, her nose nestled under the right side of my chin, hanging on to my shoulders for balance because she gets so weak in the knees. I've tried other colognes, but none of them make her fall as magically into my arms. Every woman has different "taste" in smells, but it's truly worth finding out what your lady likes, especially if you like being nuzzled by her.

5. *"Best sex ever."* No explanation required. However, this deserves a special note to the ladies reading this book: From my informal research with men, letting your husband know he has made you ecstatically happy in bed is unequivocally the most awe-inspiring, manliness-validating, "I want to take on the world!" motivating statement a wife can ever utter to a husband. Other than . . . well, I tried to come up with an other than, but quite simply, ladies, there is no other than. If you want to make your guy feel ten feet tall and leave the house walking on air, these three words should do the trick.

LOVE TO LINGER

Generally speaking . . . Americans have an inability to relax into sheer pleasure.

—ELIZABETH GILBERT

I love to relax.

—JULIO IGLESIAS

"For the past two summers I've taught a class of American college students in Spain," shared Cari Jenkins, a blogger and speaker from Denver, in an informal interview with a good friend of mine.[9] "The minute I get to Spain, everything in the world seems to slow down to a relaxed pace. It's like landing in an alternate universe. People walk slower, they seem to have time for each other, they love to linger over tapas and wine at outdoor cafes. At the coffee shops in Spain, people go there to drink coffee and gather in groups—small or large—to talk and laugh and share life. It is a culture shock to me, coming from Starbucks in the U.S., where everyone is huddled up with their favorite tech companion: a laptop, Kindle, or iPhone.

"Then there is all that gorgeous blue water around the country. The Mediterranean Sea itself seems to dictate a more leisurely pace to life. As in Italy, the mornings start slower; things shut down in the heat of the day. Meals happen sometimes at ten o'clock or eleven o'clock at night, with children up and playing after midnight, so that socializing can happen when the weather is cool outside for visiting.

"I hopped the train to London after a few weeks in Spain this summer, and when I got off the train there, I noticed—as in America—that everyone was walking fast, with a purpose, their phones to their ears. I almost felt dizzy, as if I had landed in a country where everything was moving three times as fast as it should be going."

A blogger from Matador Network, one of the world's biggest sites for travel writing, put it like this: "In the States we dig in to lunch at our desks, a power-bar on the run, fast food in the car, and get coffee to go; Spaniards almost never eat on the go and even in a big, busy city like Madrid, you'll likely attract stares if you're munching while walking down the street. Spaniards insist on making every meal, snack, and coffee break a sit-down affair, and often linger at the table afterwards to enjoy a lengthy *sobremesa*—an after-meal conversation."[10]

What is play, really, other than relaxing into a state of pleasure and lingering there for as long as you want and can? Could the less hurried pace, the love of lingering, the willingness to pause long enough to play be part of the reason why there is such a high state of sexual satisfaction in Spain? Americans know all about the joys of vacation sex, when we finally turn off our phones, laptops, and minds to relax into pleasure and take time for long talks, unhurried meals, and good sex. Could it be that our Spanish friends have figured out a way to have vacation sex year round, by adopting a more relaxed and playful state of mind?

I love the word *linger*. It's a word we don't use much anymore in American homes or marriages. But it is a state of being that Misty and I love; the feeling of having an unrushed expanse of time to be with each other is one of the greatest pleasures. We've also discovered that lingering with each other in times of emptiness, sorrow, and despair is a great healing balm.

In 2008, Misty and I were set to embark on a cruise which began in Barcelona, Spain. The city was in all-out playful mode—as if the whole population were on Red Bull (or *Toro Rojo*)—after winning the UEFA Championship tournament. We walked through the famous La Rambla Market, a sprawling, colorful food market alive with the noise of celebrators and traditional Spanish music. We sidestepped street dancers flashing black and red fabrics as they moved in perfect step and rhythm. It was a wonderful time of smiling and laughter; Misty and I soaked in the joy of the moment. That was the sweet beginning to a beautiful and joy-filled ten-day Mediterranean experience we will always treasure. Part of what we cherish is the very sacred ending to our trip, though it was one of the most painful events we have experienced together. At the conclusion of our great adventure in Spain and beyond, our joys quickly turned to confusion and sorrow, as on our final day back in the great city of Barcelona, Misty miscarried.

Instead of running through the streets for the last-minute visits and souvenir shopping we had planned before packing up for the next day's long plane ride home, we were in our hotel room. Misty was on the floor of our bathroom, doubled over in pain and protest and bleeding, gutted and heaving in the loss befalling us.

I was in shock and did not know what I could do other than to love my wife and stay with her in the pain. So that's what I did, and as it turns out, it was what she needed.

Perhaps here is a good place for me to say that there is a time for lingering to savor the happy moments with one another and to celebrate playfully, but there is also a time for lingering with each other when your hearts are breaking. During our visits to the Mediterranean, and throughout our whole marriage as well, Misty and I have experienced both kinds of lingering. On this trip in particular, there was that magical, romantic day in Naples, the day of the pizza and the sea and the kiss. But here in Spain, we experienced the kind of lingering that requires stillness and allows space for deep, wrenching grief. Where no level of historical beauty or artifacts or poetic prose holds any interest or value anymore. Where all that matters is presence. The presence of God and of spouse. And attunement.

I also want to say this: You may both be doing everything you can to bring passion and romance to your relationship, then find you are hit with an unexpected loss, a sudden death, or some other sharp edge of reality that can't be ignored. These times demand a shift in your attention, sometimes for months. But please don't think this means you aren't being passionate. Passion has many sides to it, like a diamond. Sometimes it looks like joyfully dancing in the street; sometimes it looks like holding your wife as she cries on your shoulder, and praying over her broken heart.

THE BODY BEAUTIFUL

When I say that all my women are dazzling beauties,
they object. The nose of this one is too large; the hips
of another, they are too wide; perhaps the breasts of
a third, they are too small. But I see these women for
how they truly are—glorious, radiant, spectacular,
and perfect—because I am not limited by my eyesight.
Women react to me the way that they do, Don Octavio,

because they sense that I search out the beauty that
dwells within, until it overwhelms everything else.

—DON JUAN, FROM *DON JUAN DEMARCO*

Legendary Spanish lover Don Juan got a lot of things right. He saw that a woman's true beauty comes from within and that outer beauty comes in many forms. He knew it is the eye of the beholder, as much as the subject itself, that makes up a moment of dazzling beauty.

On the other hand, there is the pesky issue of Don Juan moving from woman to woman, lover to lover, like a frisky Spanish rabbit. This is definitely not a practice that will win men any applause from their wives. In fact, the only thing it will yield is a hefty stack of divorce papers. So I am not advocating the promiscuity of Don Juan here to anyone. But I am saying that good, faithful American husbands can learn a lot from Spanish romantics about how to be a more passionate lover to their one and only beloved wife.

As she warmed to her memories of those summers in Spain, Cari (the blogger and speaker from Denver) talked about the differences between American and Spanish cultures, especially in their view of the body and beauty. "I'll tell you something that really surprised me. I feel more like a woman the minute I arrive in Spain. I feel more sensual, more feminine. They are, as a people, amazingly aware, accepting, and appreciative of the human body. Not in the way Americans are body self-conscious. They are simply body conscious, aware of the wonder of the human body, and people of all ages and sizes seem to feel comfortable and sexy in whatever skin they happen to be in. For example, you would think that since most of the beaches in Spain allow nudity, only the most perfect bodies would show up to sunbathe. But no. You see every size and shape of woman there in complete comfort, embracing her body just as it is—whether she is twenty or seventy-five, whether she is tall, short, thin, or round. Back in America, I am instantly conscious of every part of my body that is not perfect. I reach for a shrug or a sweater to cover up my upper arms, which seem suddenly too big. In Spain, I am conscious that my body, as it is, is already perfect. I wear spaghetti straps there and never think about how my arms look. I feel beautiful just because I am a woman.

"In addition, what Americans would consider flirting is just the way Spanish men and women, of all ages, talk to everyone, everywhere. There is lots of eye contact, touching, knowing smiles, laughter, intense questions, and honest confessions. I think this too adds to the feeling of sensuousness in Spain and is probably why they enjoy talking with each other so much more than staring into an iPhone. Just chatting is very entertaining there!"

Cari admitted that things were far from perfect in Spain. The economy is awful right now, and many are out of work. People are incredibly friendly and love meeting up at cafes, but it can be hard to make deep, intimate friendships. They rarely invite guests, other than family, into their homes. There's a strong distaste for the church and religion, thanks to oppressive religious dictators in the country's past, and therefore meaningful conversations about God don't happen much. No country is perfect; no one country has it all. But Spain has learned something vital about keeping passion alive and never losing your playful child-heart.

PLAYFUL ART OF DANCING

In my house . . . there was always music, and everybody was dancing. . . . Not hippie, but very free.

—PENELOPE CRUZ

I'll never forget going to meet Misty's parents in Muncie, Indiana, in the home where she had once lived as a teenager with her family. We drove onto a street that looked a lot like the street where I grew up. We pulled into the driveway of a house that also looked like the house of my youth. We walked in, and I immediately noticed that her childhood home had almost the exact same floor plan as that of my childhood home back in Texas: it was a small, ranch-style brick home with bedrooms to the right of the entrance and a living area to the left.

However, one part of this little home was glaringly different from the one I had grown up in, and I gasped when I stumbled into it. Her parents opened the door to the garage, and I knew that my childhood and Misty's were worlds apart.

> We don't stop playing because we grow old; we grow old because we stop playing.
>
> —GEORGE BERNARD SHAW

The Byrd family garage looked like a combination soda fountain and record shop. A neon Rockin' Robin sign shone above while a Wurlitzer jukebox filled the room with sounds from the 1950s and early '60s. Misty's father was a record collector and cataloger. Mike was never affluent, but over forty years he'd pay twenty-five cents for a record, or a stack of them, here and there. Flea market by flea market and garage sale by garage sale, he built his collection to more than two hundred thousand stellar records from that very special midcentury era he loved so much. Name a song from that era, and my bet is that my father-in-law could have found it, put it on his turntable, and spun you back five or six decades in a few minutes' time. And he would have crooned along to the tune while his four girls danced and laughed and doo-wopped in the background. When Mike Byrd passed away, he left his family with many precious gifts, and memories of the playful, life-giving enjoyment of music and dancing are some that my wife cherishes the most.

Remember the NewLife land cruise from the opening of this chapter? Well, there is a little more to the story of that night after I first locked eyes with Misty of the Beautiful Laugh. After my buddy John Townsend's band played a few numbers, John stepped off the stage during their next song and joined me down on the dance floor. He and I wanted to make sure that everyone in attendance got a chance to dance if they wanted to. We even found some guests in wheelchairs and spun them around, so they might feel as light on their wheels as other guests felt on their

More Benefits of Playfulness

- *Playful folks are smarter and wiser as they age.* A study conducted at Penn State focused on the elderly. It showed that playfulness in later life is associated with better cognitive and emotional functioning.

- *Playful people have less stress.* University of Illinois associate professor and playfulness expert Lynn A. Barnett says, "People who are playful don't run away from stress, they deal with it—they don't do avoidance." Because of this, they actually experience less stress overall.

- *Playful people are self-entertaining and rarely bored.* In another study, Barnett discovered that playful people were more adept at keeping themselves entertained when they were forced to sit in an empty room. "The low-playfulness people hated it. They couldn't wait to get out of there," says Barnett. The playful folks actually *enjoyed* sitting in the boring room, even though they didn't do anything the researchers could observe. "They were just in their heads—they entertained themselves," she says.

heels. It was so much fun. Then, as John jumped up to rejoin the band, a woman who had been standing near Misty mentioned to me that Misty had not yet had a turn on the floor.

I extended my hand and invited Misty to dance. Fun and brief, our moment probably seemed insignificant to any onlookers, as Misty was one of many people I danced with that night. But I never forgot it. A year later, when I was in a better place emotionally, I got the courage up to ask Misty out on a date, and we danced again.

We've not stopped dancing since.

If the music is right, we will dance in a mall, a hall, a charity ball, or anywhere we feel the rhythm and desire to move together. Back when I was in college and seminary, I loved dancing. But it was one of those hobbies that fell away as decades passed and life seemed to get more serious. Misty not only brought laughter to my life; she also revived my love for music and dancing. We often have music play in our home, so it's natural for us to dance into each other's arms, kitchen or bathroom, get into the rhythm of the song and the cadence of each other's heartbeat. The kids are used to seeing Mom and Dad fall into a swing step while dinner is cooking, or ease into a waltz while steaks are grilling on the patio. They love it, and we're now teaching them a few of our moves so they can join in on the fun.

Love is tango and tango is love! Yes, it is a dance, yet so much more than just any dance. It is an ongoing conversation between two souls, two hearts and two bodies. It is a sacred dance we enter in with one another, where both "masculine" and "feminine" feel fully expressed and honored.

—Ilona Glinarsky, dance instructor

Salsa. The tango. Flamenco dancing. Spain produced some of the world's sexiest dancing. The tango, for example, is basically a dramatic two-person play of sexual tension, set to music. It's a sexy, flirtatious dance in which your feet are going the same direction in a passionate, determined fashion but the woman's head is turned sharply away from the man's, as if to say, "You'll have to work to get my eyes and attention. You'll have to chase me, baby, if you want to catch me."

Dancing is as close to making love as you can get with your clothes and slick-soled shoes on. And the Spanish dances are all about romance, flirting, highlighting the polarity of the two sexes, the come-hither push-pull of the human mating ritual.

Which is probably part of the reason why lots of Southern Baptists who grew up in my era learned a chant that went, "I don't drink, dance, smoke, or chew—and I don't go out with girls who do." My parents were Southern Baptists who did not drink, but when it came to dancing, they couldn't say no. My father came from a family who danced. One of the sweetest memories I have of my grandparents is the day they cleared the living room at their lake home and danced a polka in perfect step with each other. My grandfather, "Dad Art," had a presence and personality much like John Wayne's. What I caught from him that night was that a Southern gentleman could be tough enough to fight for his woman but also gentle enough to dance with her.

A few years ago, I had the great privilege of filling in for Rick Warren, preaching five services in one weekend at Saddleback Church. After I preached one of the services, the mood was especially light, and the worship musicians struck up a rousing number, full of brass and drums, that set my feet to moving. I glanced at Misty, who'd been sitting in the front row. She returned my come-hither look, and we did what comes naturally. She stepped into my arms, and we began moving to a rock-step swing beat. I twirled Misty up the aisle and swung her down front in that megachurch Southern Baptist auditorium. Parishioners who were mingling on their way out of the church paused and smiled in our direction.

We could not help ourselves. When we stopped dancing, we heard spontaneous applause from many who'd lingered to watch. Somehow I think God was smiling right along with us all. Throughout all of Scripture, dancing was a part of the worship experience, as it still is in many cultures. Even babies in diapers will start bouncing and rocking to the beat of music; dance seems to be hardwired into our DNA.

> There are shortcuts to happiness, and dancing is one of them.
>
> —Vicki Baum

I love it when others get inspired by our joy of dancing and decide to take a lesson or two themselves. One couple who are friends of ours decided to take tango lessons. But because the wife kept trying to lead, the instructor had her close her eyes. She was amazed at how this allowed her to let go, trust her partner, and dance more in flow.

Dancing, like passion, is about surrendering—without fully knowing what lies ahead—to the feelings of attraction and excitement and love in our relationship. In dancing, a woman trusts her partner to lead and guide her with the smallest amount of pressure from his hands on her waist and hand, without a word. She can literally close her eyes and surrender to the music and his touch.

It requires two people being completely attuned and present in the moment, which is one of the beautiful things about dancing—all the chatter in your mind has to stop while you succumb to the sway of the music together.

LOVE OF LAUGHTER

Anyone can be passionate, but it takes real lovers to be silly.

—ROSE FRANKEN

One thing that I am proud of: I am really capable of laughing at myself.

—PENELOPE CRUZ

If you were to take a walk on a summer's eve in Spain, you would hear the sounds of music and talking, but above it all, you'd hear laughter. Spaniards love to laugh, which is a sign of a playful spirit.

When was the last time you laughed so hard that you doubled over or almost cried? Afterward, didn't you experience a wonderful feeling of having let go of stress, a sense of general well-being, a good tired? Laughing leaves us spent in the most marvelous of ways. In fact, laughter is up there with good sex for its ability to relieve stress and foster a feeling of connection between spouses.

At the beginning of this chapter, you may recall, I said that the number one trait a man desires in a woman he wants to be with over the long haul of life is that she have a sense of humor. Because I have adult ADHD, Misty's sense of humor has been one of our marriage's saving graces. Not only does she find me more amusing than irritating, but also she has a sharp wit that cracks me up on a regular basis. That helps me laugh at myself instead of get frustrated with my inability to focus. A sense of humor has helped ease so many of our adjustments to marriage and has served to both make our marriage lots of fun and add to the passion in our relationship.

It also greases the skids for our kids. A while back, our boy Carter was complaining about one of his baseball coaches at school. The coach may have known about baseball, but in regard to his coaching style, he was more like a "my way or the highway" military sergeant, sternly barking orders, shouting at the players about what to do and how they needed to do it—seven minutes ago! Never looked the kids in the eye.

Misty and I could see Carter's frustration. To help him relax, Misty encouraged Carter, "Oh, honey, I sure understand. You're just used to Steve. He's a little different from the barking type of coach. Can you imagine how Steve would do it? 'Okay, everyone, we are going to play baseball.'"

Taking a cue from Misty, I mimicked the stance of a coach about to give his team the plan. "Okay, okay, okay," I said in my best hyperactive coach voice. "It looks like we have these four bases out there. No wait, I forgot the hump in the middle. Three of you go get on the three of those bases out there, and I'll put the throwing dude on the hump in the middle. If you see the ball coming to you, get it. Catch it. Throw it. Or touch the guy running by you."

From the corner of my eye, I saw Misty starting to lose it. That's all the encouragement I needed. "Okay, now somebody jump on the hump and throw the ball to their guy with the stick. Wait, wait. Just . . . act like you're throwing it to him but trick him and make him miss. Okay, alright, okay, I need someone behind the stick man, to get down on one knee to throw the ball back to the guy on the hump. Okay, okay, now, see all that space out there behind the bases? We need three guys spread out back there. You three boys get the ball and throw it where the runner is headed. Okay, now throw it to the man with the stick, and let's see what happens!"

At this point, Misty was rolling on the floor. Carter was cracking up as well, the tension in his face replaced by can't-breathe laughter.

Once the comedy bit was over and the laughter had settled, I caught Misty looking at me in that way that said, "I love how you make us laugh." A moment later, the snickers started back up, and we were all laughing again for a second round.

Misty often tells me that laughter is a wonderful precursor for her to more intimacy with me. When couples laugh together, they are in agreement (that something is funny). Private jokes between spouses create a bond of mutual understanding and comic memories. Laughing together helps create safety, allows us to let our guard down and enjoy the pleasure of being known, flaws and all. All this is to say, men would be wise to maximize the laughter quotient in their marriage, especially if they want to increase the passion quotient.

Actress Joanne Woodward was married to heartthrob-handsome Paul Newman for fifty years before his death in 2008. When asked about their secret to lifelong attraction, she said, "Sexiness wears thin after a while and beauty fades, but to be married to a man who makes you laugh every day, ah, now that is a treat." Perhaps the greatest bargain in the world is laughter. It costs nothing, defies age, bonds you with others, makes you seem sexier than you really are, and helps everyone feel almost instantly better. And if you can make someone laugh, you win. Even when there is no competition.

WORK TO LIVE

I always knew I wanted a family, because of the way I grew up. Family has always been the most important thing.

—PENELOPE CRUZ

The people of Spain (and several other Mediterranean countries) tend to work to live; they do not live to work. I would like to think it is because they simply have their priorities straight, especially on the importance of family life.

"In Spain work fits around social and family life, not vice versa. The foundation of Spanish society is the family and community, and the Spanish are noted for their close family ties, their love of children and care for the elderly (who are rarely abandoned in nursing homes)."[11]

Because my work for NewLife and as a speaker requires me to be away from home at times, I stay connected as much as possible. I leave notes, and I will call and text while traveling. Through the modern marvel of FaceTime and Skype, we have eaten dinner together as a family when I am thousands of miles away. I'm so thankful that fun and laughter and love can be transferred over the internet when I have to be away.

Before I get home, usually while on the plane or in my hotel room, I design and write letters and cards (more on this in chapter 5) and pick up surprises for everyone. This helps me shift my focus to my family. When I arrive home, it is essential that I am truly there, in every sense of the word. This past fall was heavy with travel. I went to Ireland for ten days and then to Brazil for several days, followed by a few days in Nebraska. This meant a lot of activity and new experiences that my high-energy personality loves, but I wasn't prepared for how wiped out I'd be after all that back-to-back international travel. I couldn't wait to get home! The temptation might have been to walk in the door, share all my fascinating experiences, and then go lie down for a twenty-four-hour nap. But I've learned to put my stories from the road on hold for a few hours while I put my focus 100 percent on my love for and desire to see my wife and kids. They need to know that they are my life, my number one priority, and that no matter where I go in the world, there is one locale that matters more to me than anything, and that is a place called home.

If my work and family life get out of balance, and it has, Misty lets me know. She brings it up in a conversation and we discuss it. Then

I will realize I've veered off track, make necessary adjustments in my schedule again, and everyone's mood shifts for the better.

Guys, here's one way to test whether you are a "fun dad" to your kids: when you walk in the door after a long day or a short trip away, do your children run toward you, smiling? Or do they slink away quietly, giving you space? Those first few minutes when you enter the house are fraught with significance. Take time to greet the kids in a positive, playful way. Hug, tickle, laugh, and react with enthusiasm to whatever they want to show or tell you.

Then find that lovely wife of yours, twirl her around, maybe lower her into a fancy dance dip, and tell her, in your best Antonio Banderas accent, that her personal Don Juan has arrived to make all her dreams come true. Offer to take her upstairs and make passionate love to her—or wash some dishes or entertain the kids while she catches her breath.

Whatever you do, just do it in sincere delight in your family. Play.

Then stand back and watch the needle on the passion meter in your marriage start to rise.

Thirteen Ways to Keep Your Love Playful

———

1. Watch a movie or play together that is guaranteed to make you both laugh. A few of our favorites are *Elf*, *Ground Hog Day*, and *The Princess Bride*.

2. Choose to laugh more, criticize less. Make the family dinner table a time of laughter and fun by making it a criticism-free zone. Ask each other to share the most embarrassing experiences or the funniest or happiest moments that occurred during the week.

3. We Americans often keep our minds on fast-forward, for a variety of reasons: our work ethic, too many activities, the

culture of social media and the internet. We place a high value on efficiency and getting things done quickly. Give yourselves permission to set aside a period of time every day to slow down and linger—both alone with yourself, to spend in prayer or meditation and letting go of worries, and with each other, as a way to bless one another with your focus and presence and love. Put away the technology during these times. Think like a Spaniard and slow down.

4. Ask yourselves, "Are we living to work or working to live?" Talk about the work/life balance and ways to prioritize your life outside of work, especially if work has begun to creep up and diminish your ability to relax, play, turn off the noise in your head, and be fully present to each other.

5. If you love to dance but haven't done it for a while, consider going out for an evening of dinner and dancing. While you cook or relax at home, play music that makes you want to take your mate in your arms and tango or salsa your way round the kitchen. Or take some Latin dance lessons.

6. Become body conscious but not body self-conscious. In other words, show gratitude and appreciation for your own body by treating it well, and show your mate how much you love and appreciate their body too, with words of affirmation, a playful wink and a sexy pat, a gentle caress. Never criticize your spouse's body. Be especially careful to keep your eyes on the prize of your partner when out in public, showering them with your loving gazes. Don't look around the room or stare at other attractive people; your mate deserves your eyes to be on him or her and to feel, in your presence, that they are the most desirable person in the room.

7. Is your sex life playful? Do you take the time you need to linger before, during, and after sex, to deeply connect? (Quickies can also be playful and fun; just make sure you also make time for unhurried lovemaking.)

8. Play a game, indoor or out, that you know puts people in a playful mood. Twister, Pictionary, Taboo, and charades generally lead to some good laughs. Set up a croquet or badminton set in the backyard, where dinner on the patio can lead to some spontaneous game playing. Keep a Frisbee, a football, an oversized plastic ball and bat, a kickball, or a big bottle of soap bubbles handy in a basket on the porch for easy fun. Let yourselves play and be kids at heart again.

9. Go out to a family-friendly comedy club or improv theater. These can be a blast, and often the audience gets to participate, so it's more than passive entertainment.

10. Be an easy laugher—that is, be on the lookout for humor in life, note the everyday quirks that make humans so endearingly funny, and share them at dinner. Learn to laugh at yourself and see more of your flaws and mistakes as humorous rather than something to get anxious about. Make a habit of sharing funny quotes, cartoons, memes, or anecdotes with your mate via text, email, and Facebook during the day when you are away from each other. Send a playful, flirty text once a day to your spouse, something you know will make them smile or laugh, lift their spirits, and make them look forward to seeing you at the end of the day. Anybody can cultivate a better sense of humor!

11. Make your own romance language. Learn a few sexy or romantic phrases or terms of endearment in Spanish, Italian, or French that are just between the two of you. Also, check out your

ratio of positive to negative words in your personal vocabulary. Emphasize being more positive in your communication style to your mate and your kids; be more upbeat and enthusiastic whenever you can. This doesn't mean being fake when you are sad or struggling, but for many people, being negative has become a habit, a way of seeking sympathy or getting attention. Try being the family encourager and look for ways to build up your mate.

12. Get away to do nothing but play. Americans are amazing at turning even their vacations into opportunities to catch up on work. Get away somewhere that will force you to unplug from routine, encourage you to relax in a new environment, and most of all remind you to play! For some couples, this could be camping; for others, it means heading to the beach; for still others, it is a weekend getaway to a great online deal at a fancy hotel. It could also be as simple as going for a walk together on a nice evening, in a new neighborhood or around a new park. Doing anything new, even trying out a new restaurant, stimulates endorphins in the brain, evoking feelings of happiness.

13. Talk about favorite childhood play. What did you love doing as a kid on summer days or summer eves? How did you keep yourself entertained? Just sharing these memories can put you in a dreamy, connected, playful mood. Surprise each other with spontaneous fun. Get up off the couch, turn off the TV, and announce, "Everybody pile in the car. We're going to play minigolf (or go bowling or biking) and then get an ice cream cone!"

CHAPTER 4

THE SECRET OF SAVORING FOOD

*You feed the people nearest and dearest to you—and
you feed them well. We all know that eating can be
sensual . . . A good meal has the power to recharge a
relationship because eating can be soothing and sexually
stimulating all at the same time.*

—FRANCESCA DI MEGLIO

In a scene from the movie *Julie and Julia*, the camera opens to Paul and Julia Child dining together in a Parisian restaurant. The waiter glides to the table and serves them a filet of sole that has been baptized and simmered in brown butter. Julia takes a bite of the fish, and her expression turns to one of pure rapture. Then, in a ritual familiar to all couples who love each other and good food, she says, "You have to taste this" and feeds her husband a sampling of the exquisite dish. They are both so taken with this perfect bite that neither can put words to the experience; they manage only to mutter and sputter until Paul answers his wife's wordless, almost tearful expression of wonderment by nodding and agreeing, "I know. I know. I *know*."

In her book *My Life in France*, Julia recalled this meal, her first in Paris, as the most exciting of her life. Little did she know then that a fire of passion was being lit that would soon burst into flame and change the world of cooking for all time.

It is also one of my favorite scenes in the movie, a glimpse into how sharing sumptuous food with your love can prompt feelings of passion and connection. This short scene masterfully shows how food engages all the senses—the appetizing sight of the fish served in the copper pan it was cooked in, the tantalizing aroma (in the scene, Julia inhales the scent and dreamily pronounces it: "Butter"), the tactile sensation as the flakey meat is lifted from the bone, the sounds of sizzling, and finally the delicious taste exploding on the tongue. Food, when done well, is one of the rare treats given to humankind that can deliver a sort of "full-body experience" of ecstasy. When food is prepared with skill and love, and we take the time to delight in it together as a couple, it can drench our senses with pleasure.

> In France, cooking is a serious art form and a national sport.
>
> —PAUL CHILD, *MY LIFE IN FRANCE*

Perhaps the old saying "The way to a man's heart is through his stomach" is at least partially true. For food and love have been intertwined since the beginning of time.

One of the mysteries to Mediterranean passion is the seductive mingling of food and sensuality, pleasure, and love. Though France is most famous for producing the world's greatest chefs, Italy, Greece, Spain, and Israel are all known for their colorful, intensely flavorful dishes. And all of these countries are passionate about growing, cooking, serving, and savoring food in ways that escape the average "let's hurry up and eat" mentality of American couples.

How can learning to revel in food experiences increase the passion in your life and marriage? Let me count the ways.

GOURMET APPETITES IN THE KITCHEN AND BEDROOM

People who really enjoy food tend to be sensual . . .
It comes with the territory of taking pleasure in the
physical elements of life. One of those elements is, well,
food. But another . . . is sex. Two physical things that
keep humanity rolling. Two very basic needs, and two
very basic desires . . . both . . . should be relished.

—ZACHARY GOLDSTEIN, *THE WEEKLY NOSH*

Perhaps because there is an undeniable link between food and sex, many of the words we use regarding the two are similar: luscious, hunger, temptation, appetite, sizzling, satiated, satisfied. I think God created both food and sex to be pleasurable because, well, he loves us and wants us to taste the pure joy of multisensory human experiences. (A preview, perhaps, of heaven's bliss?) Because, yes, he is just that good. And also because there is something vitally sustaining about these experiences. We need to eat regularly to live and be healthy; couples need to come together for intimacy regularly in order to live happily and healthily in lifelong passion.

In her charming memoir *Lunch in Paris*, Elizabeth Bard wrote about falling in love and eventually marrying a Frenchman in Paris. He wooed her with food, whipping up incredibly tasty dishes with the sparsest of ingredients in a ninety-nine-cent pan in his tiny apartment. She believed that her open admiration and enjoyment of his simple gourmet cooking is part of what made her irresistibly alluring to him. She put it this way: "It's simple: Women who pick at their food hate sex. Women who suck the meat off of lobster claws, order (and finish) dessert—these are the women who are going to rip your clothes off and come back for seconds."[1]

Hmmm. Food for thought, ladies and gentlemen.

FOOD, SCIENCE, AND SEX

Seduction in Italy begins at the table as food and sex are inextricably linked.

—JODIE GRUMMOW, *ALTERNET* [2]

The overlap in the brain between food and sex is so profound that it's no surprise these two primal passions often dovetail in real life. Indeed, there are some fascinating studies that look at the link between food and sex.

Researchers have found, perhaps not too shockingly, that well-fed women are much more likely to want to have sex than hungry women. This is because the body of a woman who is fed produces the hormone leptin, which allows the sex hormones to work their magic in the brain. When a woman is hungry, leptin drops, and the hormones of desire go with it. So guys, every bite she takes helps get you closer to the bedroom. [3]

Another intriguing bit of food-sex science: when you train your brain to detect flavor nuances in wine or food, it is like cross-training. The benefits of becoming more of a gourmet cross over from the kitchen and dining room into the bedroom. "Experiencing new sensations—or finding new nuance in familiar ones—can create physical brain changes that make us more perceptive eaters and better lovers," says Adam Pack, PhD, a neuroscientist at Utica College. [4] Beverly Whipple, PhD, coauthor of *The Science of Orgasm*, agrees. "We literally taste, smell, and consume our lovers. The way the food looks, its texture, its aroma . . . all these things can spill over into your sex life, too." [5]

You may think that loving and enjoying food this much would lead to obesity and possibly put a big damper on your sex life. *Au contraire*. Researchers at Cornell University discovered that "those who had eaten the widest variety of eccentric foods, from beef tongue to kimchi, also reported high levels of physical activity, love for cooking, interest in nutrition and health, and arguably the most compelling finding, had the lowest BMIs. That's right. Those who had the greatest vested interest in food were also those within the normal healthy weight range."[6]

There is no doubt that good food is more appreciated and savored in Mediterranean countries. And yet in these nations the obesity level is lower, and the health of the population is higher, than in America. Could this be, in part, because the people of these countries respect and honor food more? In fact, could it be that the problem with American diets is not that we love food too much but that we love (and respect) it too little?

When people who consider themselves foodies practice eating Mediterranean style, by slowing down and enjoying food as one of life's great pleasures, they reap health benefits. "Self-described foodies may love food and spend an [inordinately] large portion of their day revolved around finding the newest food fad, taste bud–provoking meals, and niche restaurants, but that love is coupled with respect. They don't overdo it and, according to the recent findings, balance their meals with fitness."[7]

It only makes sense that if we alter our mindset from fast food–based eating to slower, gourmet tastes, this will spill over into other areas of our life, particularly our love life. For example, I think pornography is akin to drive-through junk food for the mind. Making love to your beloved, however, starting with flirting in the morning and ending with limbs entwined in the evening—now, that is more like a seven-course meal, God's intention for gourmet sex. Porn is fleeting and cheap, and though it may give some intense and immediate physical release, there is, beneath it, an ongoing hunger, an ache in the belly for something more. Something that deeply satisfies us body, heart, and soul. Intimate sex is rich Swiss cheese fondue on fresh, warm, crusty ciabatta. Porn is canned cheese on a cracker. One is the culmination of all the elements of Mediterranean passion. The other is the elimination of everything but momentary relief, without really satisfying what the heart is craving. We don't condone porn or manufactured cheese products.

COOKING UP PASSION

Cooking is like sex; it's about giving pleasure.

—GORDON RAMSAY

Through all the world there goes one long cry from the heart of the artist: Give me a chance to do my best.

—ISAK DINESEN, *BABETTE'S FEAST*

The award-winning foreign film *Babette's Feast* is about a French chef who escapes Paris during a dangerous civil war and is taken in by simple Norwegian sisters. They have no idea of the depths of her talent. She cooks with the ingredients they give her: lutefisk and other colorless and tasteless foods.

Then one day, Babette asks to create a feast for the sisters and her Lutheran friends. There follows scene after scene of exotic and expensive ingredients arriving by boat, including a live turtle and many bottles of the best French wine. Then the camera takes us to the kitchen, where Babette's talents as a chef are unleashed. She works happily and tirelessly behind the scenes as she cooks and serves a sumptuous meal paired with the perfect wines. As the stoic Lutherans begin to eat and sip, they are transformed and softened before our eyes by the beauty and taste of the food, the warmth of the wine in their bellies. They relax and offer forgiveness to each other for past hurts, their stiff upper lips relax into smiles, and they give God praise for this healing and joyful feast.

Toward the end of the movie, the sisters discover that Babette spent every penny of her life savings on this one meal. The sisters are heartbroken that now Babette will be poor for the rest of her life. But Babette begs to differ. "No, I shall never be poor. I told you that I am a great artist. A great artist, mesdames, is never poor. We have something, mesdames, of which other people know nothing."

The something of which Babette speaks is twofold: first, she has the gift of giving others a unique and great pleasure; second, she has been given a chance to do her very best work, to perform her artistry with food, which is, in and of itself, the ultimate pleasure. Babette insists that though her friends enjoyed a delightful meal, she received the greater pleasure from imagining, creating, cooking, and serving the meal.

When we cook with each other and for each other, with love and passion, whether it is a simple pasta from a dollar store pan or a seven-course French feast, we are performing artists, putting our creativity and talents on a plate.

When Misty and I are at home without the tyranny of the clock pushing our schedules, we love to cook together. If we hit all the right notes, we create something so delicious and aromatic, the memory lingers for days.

We've nicknamed one of our favorite dishes the Three-Hour Salad. We stand and visit and sip and laugh while we each grab a cutting board and a sharp knife and peel, chop, or dice whatever looks interesting in the fridge and pantry. The sights and smells of crisp garden veggies and savory herbs fill the kitchen with the colors and aromas of Eden. There's something inspiring about combining foods fresh from the earth, in a vivid array of hues, that feels surprisingly artistic. When salad is the main dish, we either bake or buy a loaf of bread to go with it, and the smell of that warm bread in the oven makes us feel even more like we are in a Mediterranean villa, preparing dinner together. Then we whip up our favorite dressing of lime, honey, and cilantro and drizzle it all over the chopped veggies. When we are done, the salad is a mosaic of food! And because you can munch on big salads for what seems like forever without getting full or hitting the bottom of your bowl, it feels like the whole affair—from chopping to the last bite—lasts for hours. Thus the name the Three-Hour Salad.

Over Thanksgiving we made *twelve* pumpkin pies together—from actual pumpkins. (You can imagine how the kids loved the mess!) And we're big on soups at our house. With six mouths to feed, a pot of fragrant soup simmering on the stove is easy to make, budget friendly, healthy, and delicious. And though most soups start with a good broth, everything else that goes in is limited only by your imagination and taste buds, which makes soup another fun dish to cook together. The kids too like to add a little of this and a little of that until we've made a soup as unique as the sous chefs who had a part in its creation.

DINING OUT AND DESIRE

I felt once more how simple and frugal a thing is happiness: a glass of wine, a roast chestnut, a wretched little brazier, the sound of the sea. Nothing else.

—NIKOS KAZANTZAKIS, *ZORBA THE GREEK*

Have you ever recreated a recipe—say, your mom's chicken soup—and even though you did everything technically right, you notice that it just doesn't taste the same as when she cooked it and served it with love? Part of the reason may be that love is an actual ingredient. But there's something else at play. When you cook for yourself, you tend to taste as you cook; you know everything that went into the meal. And it can be a wonderfully satisfying dish. However, when someone else cooks for you, there is an element of newness and surprise. Your palate is clean, and you tuck into the dish with anticipation, not knowing how it will taste. And when that first bite turns out to be layered with flavor, surprisingly delicious, it can be a real rush, one of life's succulent pleasures.

Ten Foods Considered to Be Natural Aphrodisiacs[8]

1. *Cinnamon:* Eating cinnamon heats up your body and, in turn, your sex drive. Cinnamon also has anti-inflammatory properties, and can help normalize blood sugar.

2. *Pine Nuts:* Loaded with zinc, which is essential for producing testosterone, pine nuts have reportedly provided men with sexual stamina since the Middle Ages. Grind them up with basil, garlic, and olive oil for a delicious pesto.

3. *Cardamom:* In the Arabian Nights, you can read of the use of this ancient spice as an aphrodisiac. The spice comes in pods, which you can grind for use as needed. Cardamom is warming and pungent, and can increase blood flow, which probably accounts for its aphrodisiac properties. [No wonder I loved this tea from the first sip!]

4. *Celery:* This crunchy, aromatic vegetable serves as a flavor base for soups and stews in cuisines around the world. It is also high in essential nutrients necessary for great sex, and it contains two chemicals—androsterone and adrostenol—which serve as a sexual attractant when ingested.

5. *Avocado:* This silky, mild fruit has a reputation as an aphrodisiac extending back to ancient Aztec times. In fact, the Aztecs called the avocado tree "Ahuacuatl," which translates to "testicle tree."

6. *Almonds:* These nuts are an ancient symbol of fertility extending back to biblical times. The sweet fragrance may also serve as a sexual attractant. [Almonds are also high in beneficial fats, fiber, and vitamin E.]

7. *Honey:* Rich in B vitamins, organic raw honey supports testosterone production, which can increase desire. It also contains the boron used in estrogen production, which is important for female desire.

8. *Ginger:* Just like chili peppers, ginger spices things up and increases circulation and body temperature. In fact, legend says famous French courtesan Madame du Barry provided ginger to all of her lovers to increase their desire and improve their pleasure.

9. *Chocolate:* Pure, dark chocolate has a centuries-old reputation

as an aphrodisiac. Chocolate contains phenylethylamine (PEA), which stimulates the same hormone your body releases during sex. It also sparks dopamine production in the brain. It doesn't take much. Try a square or two of low-sugar, vegan dark chocolate.

10. *Red wine:* In moderation, red wine increases blood flow, relaxes you, and lowers inhibitions. Have a few ounces of red wine, but don't overdo it.

The element of pleasurable surprise is one of the reasons why couples often feel passion rising for each other when they go out to eat. Dining out gives us all kinds of opportunities to turn up the romance in our marriage. Misty and I not only love to cook; we also love to eat. We try to eat where there is live music, to double the pleasure. We don't order a dish. We have a little buffet at our table and sample everything we can, often ordering off the appetizer menu. There is just a little added excitement to eating when you get to eat out.

Do you remember the first dinner date you had with your spouse, before you were married? If you close your eyes, can you go back there in your memory, remember how your date looked across the table, what you ordered to eat, what you said, the atmosphere, and even the waiter? I will never forget my first date with Misty Byrd. Every detail of that dinner is etched in my memory, probably because I went over it again and again in my mind for days and weeks later.

At the time, I lived in Southern California and Misty lived in Indiana. We'd been corresponding by email for months. (I have a book of those emails, printed and bound. It's about six inches thick. Obviously, we had a lot to say!) We graduated to talking on the phone for a couple more months. So by the time Misty arrived at the airport in Orange County for our first face-to-face date, the air was thick with anticipation. (Have I mentioned that the sight of her there in baggage claim took my breath away? She looked even prettier than I'd remembered her at the fire pit on the fake cruise.)

We drove to one of the nicest restaurants in Laguna Beach, called Studio, and were seated outside in a spot overlooking the ocean, so close to the waves that we could hear them crashing on the sand below. Just a few feet from where we sat, Lucille Ball and Desi Arnaz had filmed scenes of the movie *The Long, Long Trailer* in 1953. (The restaurant had been a trailer park back in the fifties.) The waiter told us that the two palm trees towering above our heads had been named Lucy and Ricky. (Later that week, I'd end up buying a painting of Lucy and Ricky—the trees, not the famous couple—from the restaurant, as a memento of a special dinner I never wanted to forget.)

After chatting awhile and smiling a lot, we looked over the menu. At this point in my life, I'd given up eating red meat for almost twenty years. To my surprise, this delicate lady looked up, her blue eyes sparkling with joy, and ordered a steak. Not quiche, not a lovely linguine. No small, delicate dish for Misty. She was who she was, liked what she liked, and this Indiana girl wanted a nice, juicy steak. When Misty offered me a bite of that steak, I gave in to the moment and broke a two-decade beef fast. It was worth every flavorful, tender, well-seasoned, perfectly grilled bite. To this day, a good bite of perfectly cooked steak transports me to that enchanted evening, and the memories of feeling as young as a teen boy, falling in love with Misty all over again.

GROCERY DATES

"My parents go on dates—to the grocery store," writes Italian American blogger Francesca Di Meglio. "I know what you're thinking: How can *that* count as a date? But I must admit that whenever rain arrives and mamma knows that papa will have to come home early from work (he's a landscaper), she gets flushed with excitement. 'We're going to go to the market,' she says to me as though she is five and it's Christmas Eve. This hardly seems like a romantic night on the town. But for my parents, it is. Sometimes, mamma holds papa's hand in the car just as he's about to rev the engine. They listen to their favorite Italian CDs. And they treat themselves to the best—filet mignon or Asiago cheese. On these days, they are all smiles (and we all win when dinner is served). Delicious sweet love!"[9]

I loved this peek into a long-married Italian couple finding fun and passion by just going to the market together!

Misty and I love going to the nearby, colorful Saxony Farmer's Market on Saturdays—there's not only local farm-fresh produce but also artisanal foods and lively music. Another place we love to go to get inspiration for a meal is what I call the Euro-Asian-Pan-American-Vietnamese Superstore. It's a sensory wonderland for foodies. We love just picking interesting, exotic new ingredients we've never tried before. It adds an element of surprise and fun-of-discovery to cooking. Why not, at least occasionally, make an adventurous date out of finding and gathering new foods for a special meal or two?

I remember the first time I discovered saffron in one of our local international food markets. This spice, more than 3,500 years old, has always been one of the rarest and most sought-after spices. And there some saffron sat, in its golden threads of splendor, in a one-quart bag. We could not resist buying a quart of gold that can turn even plain white rice into a dish fit for royalty. And cardamom. Have you tasted cardamom? (It's also fun to say three times really fast.) When I tasted my first sip of cardamom tea, I said goodbye to my old faithful Earl Grey and welcomed this new flavor that I suddenly could not live without. It's a little bit citrusy, a little bit warm—one of the spices you find in chai tea. I love the combination of saffron rice, cardamom tea, and warm, garlic-infused naan bread. For very little money, you can enjoy an amazing spice-feast for which your taste buds will thank you! When you're exploring new spices, fragrances, and the deep flavor from freshly cooked foods, it gets easier and easier to pass by fast-food drive-throughs. You can go home and throw together a minifeast in less time, and for far less money, than you'd spend on a preformed burger and greasy fries. Just one more way to show that when you enjoy and value good food more, letting yourself become a bit of a passionate, adventurous gourmet, your diet naturally gets balanced and healthier, and it doesn't feel at all like deprivation.

SERVING UP COMPASSION

*When we find ourselves coping with pain, the kitchen
can become our therapist, food our source of comfort.*

—MIKA BRZEZINSKI, "THE PASTA CURE"

You may recall that at the beginning of this book, I spoke of how passion can take the form of compassion in long-term marriages. Cooking a meal and serving it to someone who is hungry or hurting or both has, since the beginning of time, been a way to share tangible love with others.

In the book *We Laugh, We Cry, We Cook*, my friend Becky shares the following story about cooking for her husband, Greg.

> Greg hadn't eaten lunch, and now famished, he looked up at me and then back at the plate of spicy catfish, oven-blistered potato slices and fresh coleslaw I had cooked and was offering him and said, "You saved my life."
>
> "Just by serving you dinner?" I asked.
>
> "Yes," he said with deep conviction.
>
> . . . I know Greg was exaggerating when he said, "You saved my life," but if you've ever been really hungry after a long day, and someone has greeted you with a hug and hot meal, it can feel pretty close to life-saving. Perhaps it is no wonder that Jesus spoke of how when we feed others who are hungry—literally and figuratively—we are feeding him too. A cup of cold water or a steaming bowl of soup, served with love . . . is no small thing.[10]

The first time I visited Misty in her home in Indiana, she prepared for me her favorite belly-warming, farm country dish: chunky potato soup. Butter, salt, pepper, milk, broth, carrots, onion, celery, cheese, and potato never tasted so good. Like warm liquid velvet. And of course what made the soup taste especially delicious and comforting was that someone I was falling in love with had prepared it just for me. And you guessed it: I never taste a good potato soup without being transported back to Misty's kitchen and all the warm feelings of comfort, caring, and love that surrounded me that day.

John Tagliabue had met and married his wife, Paula Butturini, an American-born Italian, when they were both journalists in Rome. Their love blossomed over meals they cooked and shared with each other in small apartment kitchens in Italy.

Then, in 1987, they both went to cover stories in war-torn Poland. In her memoir *Keeping the Feast*, Paula describes this as the time when the warm, happy love story turned cold and terrifying. While in the middle of riots in Prague, Paula was beaten severely. A few weeks later, John was shot and almost died from his wounds.

They eventually were able to return to Italy, but they were both suffering from the effects of the extreme trauma. Paula found that cooking became her source of comfort, and in John's painful state of mental exhaustion, eating was one of the few things he could still do and enjoy. So she dove into the daily ritual of cooking food and feeding John with all the passion she could manage, and slowly mealtimes became the thing that would tether them again to life and to each other.

Paula writes in her book, "So tonight and all the other nights when I may be tired, without appetite, or simply not in the mood to produce even a simple meal, I shall will myself to do it anyway." She describes the detailed and mouth-watering process of pairing hot spaghetti with freshly cooked clams in their own broth, adding garlic and butter and topping it all with fresh parsley. Then she continues, "I will rush the warm bowl to the dining room and then John and Julia [her daughter] and I, suddenly hungry from the sweetly pungent smell of garlic and clams coming from the kitchen, will sit down to eat. The three of us will be quiet for a moment or two as we twirl our spaghetti into the first near forkfuls that we lift to our mouths. We will chew that first bite hungrily and perhaps, if I have hit all the measurements right, give a tiny sigh of delight. Then, already heartened, we will start to talk and laugh and eat in earnest, keeping the feast that we are meant to keep, the feast that is our life."[11]

This ritual of cooking beautiful food and eating it together in the company of dear friends, every day, over time, loosened the depression and assuaged the feeling of being emotionally frozen. While I am writing this chapter on food and love in Mediterranean countries, the world is reeling from a terrorist attack in the most visited city in the world: Paris. As I read portions of *Keeping the Feast* this week, it struck me as remarkable how simple, angst-free, comforting rituals—plus old-fashioned rest, sunshine, warmth, time, a couple of good friends—can heal traumatized people, and nations. Paris will also likely begin to heal one steaming cafe au lait, one fresh baguette, one glass of red wine, one compassionate prayer, one kind word, and one tender hug at a time.

As M. F. K. Fisher, the popular American food writer, said, "There is communion of more than bodies when bread is broken and wine is drunk." Indeed, when we offer a warm mug of coffee or a hot bowl of soup to our beloveds, we may be feeding their souls. It may be passion of the quiet, gentle variety. But don't underestimate its strength to bond a couple and to help heal wounds, big and small, over a lifetime.

MEALS THAT LINGER IN OUR MEMORIES

The more our senses are engaged in an event, the deeper the memory lodges in our brain. In the book I referenced earlier, *We Laugh, We Cry, We Cook*, the authors write about this brain-food-memory connection. "Maybe that's why there are so many hidden layers of meaning when we stir a pot of Mama's chili or cut into a ripe, red watermelon and find our minds transported to picnics in the hot verdant summers of childhood. Cooking engages every sense, the taste of homemade peach ice cream, the smell of sweet corn, the sounds of steak sizzling on the grill, the hard, smooth feel of a crisp apple in the hand, the arresting beauty of fresh garden veggies artfully arranged on the lopsided ceramic plate you made at age nine. Unlike anything else, food sears itself into our memories. That's why when we feed others, we nourish them in a myriad of surprising and memorable ways."[12]

What meal do you remember most fondly sharing together as a couple? What was the food, the music, the scenery, the sounds? What made it so special that even now you can go back in time to that day, that meal, and reexperience it in your mind, as if it happened yesterday? Now, how can you use this knowledge to increase the passion in your marriage and give your soul mate a lasting memory to cherish and ponder?

Mediterraneans seem to produce memorable romantic meals almost effortlessly, and they do it often. Perhaps this is why their relational bonds tend to be so deep and wide and strong.

The meal that takes Misty and me right back to the Mediterranean hills and valleys is minestrone. In California we found a restaurant, the Pomodoro, that had minestrone like the soup we love so much in Rome, tasting of liquid paradise. When we moved to Indianapolis, we discovered that Maggiano's also had a great minestrone, and so it became our place to soothe those Mediterranean cravings.

On a special end-of-decade birthday for Misty, I promised to treat her to her favorite Italian *zuppa*. At Maggiano's, I guided her through the restaurant and toward a door near the back. When I opened it, about thirty friends and family members started singing "Happy Birthday" to my wife, whose mouth was wide open in shock and surprise. I'd hired a DJ for the occasion, so we had lots of music, along with Italian food and dancing. At one point, the DJ cued up a track to a timeless love song made popular by Johnny Mathis, "Misty." It was an evening I cherish, a bit of Italy in Indiana—music, dancing, laughter, and friends, the joys of Mediterranean sensual living right here at home.

OPENING YOUR TABLE TO OTHERS

Music, laughter, and the happy clinking of tableware
would fill the air, leaving all of us with a sense that the
world was a magnificent place.

—RAELEEN D'AGOSTINO MAUTNER, *LIVING LA DOLCE VITA*

There was a time when people entertained others, welcomed drop-in company, and had dinner parties as a way of life. Houses had front porch swings, and people sat on them and visited with the neighbors, often sharing a glass of lemonade or iced tea along with the news of the day. Somewhere along the way, Americans went inside their homes and closed their doors. The buzzword *cocooning* became a popular way to describe the desire to huddle up at home. But we also became more isolated, more in touch with technology than with each other, face-to-face, human to human.

Couples who isolate themselves this way, I believe, are missing out on a fabulous opportunity to minister to others as a team, side by side, in the casual and warm environment of their home. When Misty and I work together to invite people over and plan and create a dinner to share with them, it doesn't just bless the guests we serve; we are also blessing our marriage. For few things are as bonding or meaningful as using our shared talents to bless those who come through our front doors for a memorable meal.

THE LOST ART OF DINNER CONVERSATION

More and more, when Misty and I go out to eat, we see couples with their iPhones in hand, talking to other people virtually rather than focusing on each other face-to-face. We have fallen prey at times as well. It is so easy to keep clicking to get one more piece of information, one more bit of current news, another post on Facebook, to catch up on "connecting," all the while missing the person in front of us. It seems that as a society, we are gradually losing the art of delightful and interesting conversation with each other over a meal. Good conversation is what keeps Mediterraneans lingering for hours at the table with one another. What do they talk about? Well, for one thing, especially in France, they do not discuss problems or negative topics over a meal. It's an unspoken rule that conversations should be interesting and uplifting. (Have you ever tried to eat when someone at the table is upset or goes off on a political rant? Your digestion slows down and stops when dinner conversations become awkward and unpleasant.) What Mediterraneans love to talk about most is ideas. Philosophy. Meaning. Culture. Observations. Topics that everyone at the table can weigh in on. Mediterraneans are raised to be conversationalists and to discuss topics of depth, meaning, and interest.

"Good conversation is as stimulating as black coffee and just as hard to sleep after," wrote Anne Morrow Lindbergh. And yet many couples are so conversationally lazy that they can put each other to sleep by (1) not talking at all or (2) talking on and on about things that hold no interest for their mate.

Think of the people you have most enjoyed talking with over the course of your life. What was it about them that pulled you into the conversation and kept your interest? Misty and I discussed this and realized that the friends with whom we most like to converse show a sincere interest in us and in our thoughts and opinions; they laugh easily and add humor of their own; they are good storytellers without being long-winded or dominating or sounding as if they were onstage when they share; they are vulnerable and open and real; they are readers and thinkers; they are curious and interested in life and in others; they are growing spiritually and want to do something to make the world a better place; they are aware of their strengths and weaknesses, their successes and failures, and this makes them nonjudgmental and full of grace. Making this list together helped us see why we enjoy talking with one another over a meal, and it helped us identify a few ways each of us could up our conversational game. Try going out to dinner with your mate as if you were dining with someone you didn't know but would love to get to know better. What you discover may surprise you!

Ten Questions to Ask Your Partner at the Dinner Table[13]

Don't ask them all at once! Just pick one or two at a time.

1. If you were by yourself and could do anything you wanted for one day, what would you do?
2. What is your most vivid childhood memory?
3. If you could wake up tomorrow and have one new ability or talent, what would it be?
4. What advice would you give your younger self?
5. What do you hope people think when they think of you?
6. If you have kids: What's the most important thing you hope your kids take with them out into the world?
7. Who has been kindest to you?
8. If you could hold on to just one memory for the rest of your life, what would it be?
9. When you imagine yourself at eighty years old, what do you see?
10. What are you most grateful for?

Perhaps you've never considered the possibility that savoring food, becoming more of a gourmet in the kitchen, could increase your happiness in marriage and in the bedroom. (I told you this book would be fun, didn't I?) I hope this chapter has opened your eyes to ways that food, cooking, and serving can add up to more passion in your life and with each other.

Bon appetit!

A loaf of bread, a jug of wine, and thou.

—OMAR KHAYYAM

Thirteen Ways to Treat Your Lover
to Fun Food Experiences

1. Serve your mate breakfast in bed or tea and a snack on a pretty tray. Something that says "I love you" in a tangible way through food.

2. Put on some music and light a candle for dinner tonight, even if dinner is tacos or burgers.

3. Put together a romantic picnic of cheese and crackers and wine, perhaps stopping at a gourmet deli to pick up some interesting salads. Surprise your partner at work, or if the day is pretty, go out for a weekend drive to a park or lake.

4. Take a cooking class together. For added romance, choose a class that will teach you how to make a dish from France, Italy, Spain, Greece, or Israel—one of the Mediterranean countries known for passion.

5. Go out for tapas or appetizers and try some dishes you've not tried before. There's a great tapas restaurant in Scottsdale, Arizona, overlooking a pretty canal, that has flamenco dancing one night every week. It's called Tapas Papa Frita. Find a restaurant in your area that provides entertainment along with your meal. It's a wonderful, budget-friendly way to awaken all your senses for the cost of a meal for two.

6. Plan an old-fashioned dinner party, inviting one or two other couples whose company you both enjoy. Remember, this is about enjoying yourselves, so keep it simple, ask your guests to bring side dishes, or do whatever will make this stress free and fun!

7. Go together to a farmer's market or specialty ethnic store and plan a meal based on the foods that look most appetizing to you. Try at least one new food or spice or herb!

8. Plant a garden together. This can be as simple as a small herb garden you plant indoors in a nice window or as big as a full-blown country vegetable garden. If space is an issue, search for "space-saving gardens" on the internet, and you'll find dozens of ways to grow produce on the smallest of plots.

9. Ramp up your conversational game. The next time you go out to eat, think ahead about some good questions, interesting topics, or uplifting stories or funny facts you've heard or read. Don't forget to listen attentively and ask follow-up questions or compliment your mate's answers. Talk less about problems and more about solutions, less about negative happenings and more about positive experiences.

10. Create your own daily happy hour. Signal the end of the workday and beginning of the evening together by sitting down with a beverage (wine, hot tea, lemonade, or sparkling water, maybe) and perhaps a few nuts or cheese slices or some fruit or veggies. Turn on some soft music if you like. Ask each other about the highlights of the day, and offer a sympathetic ear to any problems or hurts that your spouse may have experienced that day.

11. Take turns researching a new ethnic cafe or restaurant to try each month. To save money, you can share a meal or enjoy half-price appetizers at happy hour or just go for dessert and coffee. Even the priciest restaurants have specials, and if you share a plate or order soup and appetizers, you can enjoy amazing tastes in beautiful places on a budget.

12. Create a meal using as many "aphrodisiac foods" as you can, just for fun!

13. Determine to slow down and enjoy your meals together, pay attention, be fully present. Flirt liberally.

CHAPTER 5

THE SECRET OF
ENJOYING BEAUTY

Much of my crying is for joy and wonder rather than
for pain. A trumpet's wailing, a wind's warm breath,
the chink of a bell on an errant lamb, the smoke from a
candle just spent, first light, twilight, firelight. Everyday
beauty. I cry for how life intoxicates. And maybe just a
little for how swiftly it runs.

—MARLENA DE BLASI, *A THOUSAND DAYS IN VENICE*

I was raised in the middle of nowhere, out in West Texas. You could go
your whole life without experiencing beauty there. Birds sit on tele-
phone poles because they are prettier than the trees. Bees die trying to
pollenate plastic flowers stuck in pseudo-gardens around houses. It is so
arid, there are more tumbleweeds than flowers, more dust storms than
raindrops. There are some locals who will argue with me, I am sure:
people who think mesquite trees are pretty, who wax eloquent about the
sunsets over cow pastures that reach into forever, who think red dirt is
artistic. I'm happy for them. It's just not my thing.

What this void of beauty did for me was give me an even deeper
appreciation for beauty wherever it can be found. Misty and I have

talked about how important beauty is to us, so we fill our home with music, paintings, and flowers. We also camp, sit by a lake, jog, walk, ski, and do our best to live our lives surrounded by natural beauty whenever possible. I am convinced it is one of the reasons why our marriage is rich with passion, even as we are busy in the nitty-gritty of raising a houseful of children. We find that when we refill our depleted tanks with beauty, it inspires us to better love life and appreciate each other.

The things that are typically described as beautiful—art, music, the human form, home decor, natural scenery, and even pleasing aromas—have one thing in common: they enter through our five senses and evoke feelings, memories, and moods that seem to bypass conscious, logical processing (the brain's prefrontal cortex). Beauty, absorbed through our senses, goes straight to the emotional center of our brain (the limbic system), enhancing our moods and creating the conditions for loving encounters, without our having a single conscious thought about it. We have all experienced how a few strains of music can evoke emotions of melancholy or romance or joy, how the aroma of cinnamon and vanilla can make us feel cozy and comforted, how a gorgeous painting or sculpture can evoke feelings of awe and inspiration, how sitting around a campfire's glow can put us in a nostalgic or romantic mood, how watching the sunset over a lake or the ocean can make us feel connected to each other by wonder.

When we see or hear something beautiful, the experience opens our heart and transports us to serene and happier states of mind, leaving us refreshed in spirit and inclined to be more generous to others, cutting them slack and giving more grace. In fact, we will discover in this chapter that natural and cultural beauty in our surroundings can have the same effect on lovers that the sun has on flowers, opening people up, like petals, to receive warmth and light. Then, with open hearts, they are ready to give each other love.

By surrounding yourselves with beauty, in all its forms, you can profoundly ignite feelings of passion and romance. Aristotle said, "Beauty is the gift of God." Indeed. It is especially a gift to couples longing to reexperience the spark of romantic passion.

In this chapter, we will focus on finding and enjoying beauty in nature, in culture and in our homes, and in the human form, particularly in your wife. The countries along the Mediterranean are famous for their beautiful countrysides, sculptures, and architecture, and the people there are known for creating simple beauty in their home environments and for celebrating physical beauty as well. It is not surprising, then, that couples go to the romance countries to surround themselves with all aspects of beauty, creating the perfect conditions for falling in love with each other again and again.

BEAUTY IN NATURE

Was she really going to live in this for a whole month?
Up to now she had had to take what beauty she could
as she went along, snatching at little bits of it when she
came cross it—a patch of daisies on a fine day … a
flash of sunset between two chimney pots. She had never
been in definitely, completely beautiful places.

—LOTTIE, *THE ENCHANTED APRIL*

The Enchanted April, Elizabeth von Arnim's novel from the early 1920s (made into a marvelous film in the early '90s), opens with the story of two life-weary English wives who have, each in her own way, put their happiness on hold for the purpose of being especially good, sacrificing wives. They've honored the needs of others so far above their own that their hearts have shriveled, like starving waifs, orphaned by their own lack of self-care. In addition, they were both neglected and taken for granted by husbands with severely misplaced priorities. "For years she had been able to be happy only by forgetting happiness," the author describes one of the ladies. "She wanted to stay like that. She wanted to shut out everything that would remind her of beautiful things, that might set her off again longing, desiring."

For this is what beauty does when we happen upon it: it awakens desire, particularly desire for sharing happiness with someone we love, who loves us in return.

On a grey, drippy London day, one of the main characters, Lottie, opens a copy of the *Times* and reads an advertisement: "To Those Who Appreciate Wisteria and Sunshine. Small mediaeval Italian castle on the shores of the Mediterranean to be let furnished for the month of April."[1]

Lottie's heart begins to pound. What would it be like to experience such beauty? Not to mention the respite from her life of constant duty and service to her exacting husband? After much handwringing and debate, Lottie and her new friend, Rose, decide to use their personal savings to rent the villa, along with two other women, boldly leaving their husbands behind in England to fend for themselves. The ladies arrive in Italy in the dead of a rain-drenched night, but with the help of the Italian staff, they find their way to their rooms and fall fast asleep.

The next morning, Lottie wakens refreshed, and after a few minutes of luxuriating in her new surroundings, she runs to her bedroom window and throws open the shutters. What she beholds there goes straight to her soul.

"All the radiance of April in Italy lay gathered together at her feet. The sun poured in on her. The sea lay asleep in it, hardly stirring. Across the bay the lovely mountains, exquisitely different in colour, were asleep too in the light."[2] Lottie can only stand and stare as she tries to take it all in. "Such beauty; and she was there to see it. Such beauty; and she alive to feel it. Her face was bathed in light. Lovely scents came up to the window and caressed her. A tiny breeze gently lifted her hair . . . How beautiful, how beautiful. Not to have died before this . . . to have been allowed to see, breathe, feel this."[3]

In these moments, face-to-face with pure beauty, Lottie feels something else stirring deep within. "It was as though she could hardly stay inside herself, it was as though she were too small to hold so much of joy, it was as though she were washed through with light."[4] Her mind wanders back home to her husband in England, the man she has seen as mostly self-centered and dull. But now Lottie sees him too, in her mind's eye, awash in this transformative, shimmering light. "She simply could not see him as he was. She could only see him resolved into beauty . . . and she found herself blessing God for her creation, preservation, and all the blessings of this life, but above all for His inestimable Love; out loud, in a burst of acknowledgement."[5]

All this bliss, this new generosity of unconditional love for her mate, this gratitude to her Creator, from a few moments of standing in a villa window, doing nothing but absorbing the beauty of the Italian seaside.

The villa's beauty works its power first on Lottie and then, one by one, on the hearts of all the women who come to the castle. As each begins to absorb the loveliness of their surroundings, as they rest and refresh themselves in the lap of nature, they in turn begin to see the best in others, to see the hurt beneath each other's flaws, and to offer grace in its place. The warm sun and azure sea seem to elevate their ability to view each other from a higher perspective, to imagine the whole of their hidden stories and offer love and understanding, whereas before they'd have felt irritable and put upon, or put out.

The castle itself, called San Salvatore ("the Savior"), becomes a Christ figure in the novel, wooing and embracing its inhabitants until they become, as a result, changed—softened and widened of heart—by divine love, through the vehicle of nature's beauty. Eventually Lottie invites her husband to join her in the beautiful Italian countryside, not wanting him to miss the magic of the place and its transforming effect. He arrives and can't help but notice his wife's changes, and he begins to see her with new and more appreciative eyes. Their love and passion rekindled, they feel like newlyweds again.

Misty and I were blessed to live in a miniversion of San Salvatore for a while after we married. It was a small home, just twelve hundred square feet, built in the art deco era of the 1920s (same time frame as that of *The Enchanted April*). Sitting just off the Pacific coast, its windows opened to sand as white as snow, which led to the ocean, whose shades of blue varied from turquoise to deep navy throughout the day. The home was built in the middle of a 1920s-style garden, where, in the spring, huge, purple blooms of fragrant wisteria draped over twenty-foot-tall hedges. Though it was a tiny home, it was full of history and compact beauty.

Our small home was a testament that beauty does not have to be found in palatial mansions worth millions of dollars. This little gem was one of the cheapest houses on the block and certainly one of the smallest. When we reluctantly decided to sell our tiny Pacific "San Salvatore" and create our home in Indiana to raise our family, there was a bit of heartache in the letting go, but the memories linger. And we've had a lot of fun importing what we can of the beauty of our California home and of the Mediterranean into our home here in the Midwest. No matter where you live, no matter how small the house or how limited the budget, decorating and surrounding your home with beautiful, personal touches will lift your spirits and increase your passion.

It is a big plus on the passion front if you can live in a beautiful natural setting or get to one regularly on foot or by bicycle. The transformative power of nature's beauty goes beyond romantic novels set in Mediterranean locales. Research on the power of nature shows that our brains are "wired to fire" in relaxed pleasure when exposed to beautiful scenes in nature—the perfect state for feeling in love with life and with each other.

Here are some of the amazing things that natural beauty does to enhance our lives.

1. *Nature is healing.* Being in nature, or even viewing scenes of nature, reduces anger, fear, and stress and increases pleasant feelings. Exposure to nature not only makes us feel better emotionally; it contributes to our physical well-being, reducing blood pressure, heart rate, muscle tension, and the production of stress hormones. Some studies indicate it may even prolong life.

    There was a classic study in which several patients underwent gallbladder surgery; half had a view of trees, and half had a view of a wall. According to the physician who conducted the study, Robert Ulrich, the patients with the view of trees tolerated pain better, appeared to nurses to have fewer negative effects, and spent less time in the hospital.

Even plants and flowers are uplifting and healing. Research done in hospitals, offices, and schools has found that even a simple plant in a room can have a significant impact on stress and anxiety. Having flowers around the home and office greatly improves people's moods and reduces the likelihood of stress-related depression. Flowers and ornamental plants increase levels of positive energy and help people feel secure and relaxed.

2. *Nature is calming.* God created us to be engrossed by trees, plants, water, and other nature elements; we are absorbed by scenes in nature and distracted from our pain and discomfort. (Have you ever been mesmerized by watching fish in a pond or a tank, the glow of a fire, the lure of a sunrise or sunset? Natural beauty can have a hypnotic, pain-lessening effect on the brain.) Healthy distractions allow our brain and body a chance to rest from looping negative thoughts.

3. *Nature is restorative.* Nature positively affects our well-being. In one study in *Mind*, 95 percent of people interviewed said that after they spent time outside, their mood improved, and instead of feeling depressed, stressed, and anxious, they began to feel more calm and balanced. Other studies show that spending time in nature or viewing scenes of nature is associated with a positive mood and psychological well-being, a sense of meaningfulness, and vitality.

One of my favorite historical figures is Duke Kahanamoku from Hawaii, the man who brought surfing to the forty-eight states, beginning in Laguna Beach. I met Duke's biographer on Oahu one day, and he signed for me a copy of a beautiful book with this iconic Olympian on the cover. Though Duke was a surfer, what he and his family loved to do most was just sit and look off into the ocean for hours and hours, mesmerized by its beauty. They all lived a long time, too. So whenever I get caught up in gazing at the gorgeous, I just write it off as extending my life expectancy.

4. *Nature helps us to focus.* Time spent in nature or simply viewing scenes from nature increases our ability to pay attention. Nature provides a much-needed break for overactive minds (like mine!), refreshing us for new tasks. Studies have shown that being outside improves memory and attention span by 20 percent. (Ornamental plants in the home help in these areas as well.)

   Children with ADD or ADHD benefit from time outside and learning in a natural environment. Being around nature can help them to engage more in the classroom, improving their focus and concentration on the task at hand. The soothing effects of natural beauty help to minimize the distractions that would otherwise occupy their minds.

5. *Nature ignites feelings of connection.* According to a series of field studies at the Human-Environment Research Lab, time spent in nature connects us to each other and to the larger world. Another study found that urbanites who had trees and green space around their building reported "knowing more people, having stronger feelings of unity with neighbors, being more concerned with helping and supporting each other, and having stronger feelings of belonging than tenants in buildings without trees."

   These feelings of belonging added up to some impressive measurable results as well: less crime, lower levels of violence and aggression between domestic partners, and better ability to cope with stress. Extended exposure to nature and wildlife increases people's compassion for each other.

6. *Nature fosters optimism.* Because of the greater number of hours spent in front of some kind of technological screen, we are suffering from what some researchers are calling "nature

deprivation." Less time in nature and more time in front of TVs and computers yields higher rates of depression. In fact, new studies are showing that too much screen time can make us cynical: too much screen time is associated with a loss of empathy and a lack of altruism. In a 2011 study published in the *Journal of the American College of Cardiology*, time in front of a screen was associated with a higher risk of death. (And this was true even for people who exercised regularly.)[6]

7. *Nature energizes us.* Research from the *Journal of Environmental Psychology* showed that being outside in nature "makes people feel more alive," and this feeling of passionate vitality happens above and beyond the effects of physical activity and social interaction. In fact, just twenty minutes in nature was enough to significantly boost vitality levels.[7]

BEAUTY IN CULTURAL ARTS

In the classic romantic movie *Moonstruck*, Nicholas Cage's character, Ronny Cammareri, is a tortured, angst-filled soul who falls in love with Cher's matter-of-fact character, Loretta. Both come from big, traditional Italian families living in New York City. Loretta is wildly attracted to Ronny too, but she is engaged to his safe, boring, oft-distracted brother Johnny. Afraid to follow her heart, she decides to do her duty by Johnny and go forward with their wedding plans. Ronny is heartbroken at Loretta's choice to deny the love burning between them, but he has one last request: he asks Loretta to accompany him for an evening at the opera.

Dressed to the nines, the two meet at the Metropolitan Opera House, and though Loretta is breathtakingly gorgeous in a red silk dress and heels, she is resolved to keep the evening platonic. However, as the moving and tragic opera (*La Boheme* by Puccini) plays on stage, as the orchestra swells and the magnificent voices hit passionate crescendos, Loretta's resolve melts away. She's transported—by the beauty of music and story—out of her tough, practical shell and into a realm of possibilities in which all that truly matters is love. She ends up in Ronny's arms that night, eventually admitting to herself and her family that, logical or not, she loves her fiance's brother "somethin' awful."

Such is the power of the arts to bypass our mental walls and sneak up on our hearts. When we share these art-inspired, transcendent moments with each other, our hearts are laid open by beauty. Deep connection and passion is often the result.

THE BEAUTY OF MUSIC

One of the most common triggers to feelings of passion is listening to romantic music. Most of us fell in love with music of some kind playing in the background.

What songs, when you hear them, make you reach for your spouse's hand in knowing remembrance of the time you fell in love?

Misty and I had our first encounter dancing to a swinging version of "Rock This Town" played by John Townsend's band. Soon the songs of the fifties that Misty grew up on filled our home: "Moonlight in Vermont," "Chances Are," "You Send Me," "You Belong to Me," and "Someone to Watch Over Me." Songs that are easy on the ears and great for a spontaneous slow dance. We will dance to anything, but perhaps the song I love to dance to most is her song, "Misty." (And indeed I get misty just imagining her in my arms, this music playing.) In my depression before meeting my wife, I had grown tone deaf in more ways than one. She brought music back to my life.

Because of our love for music, we pick out and play music to provoke feelings of love, of calm, of passion when we go on a road trip or have a hotel getaway. When we go out to eat, we often choose a spot where there is live music, and we want to be as close to it as possible, preferring to take a table in the bar by the pianist rather than a faraway booth in the main dining area. We've found that hotel restaurants in our area will often entertain their guests with live music, so we become their guests for an hour or two, listening, hors d'oeuvreing, and dancing. Have you ever created compilations or playlists of your favorite love songs for each other? If not, create one together or maybe make one as a surprise for a special occasion.

BEAUTY OF ART AND CULTURE

In addition to music, Misty and I love art and culture in all forms! Besides visiting art museums, we've also filled our home with art, and most of it is art we have created rather than purchased. (More on that in the next chapter.) Friends and family know of my love for art, which is why, on one of my big end-of-decade birthdays, I found myself on a party bus to the Museum of Contemporary Art, in Chicago. At the time, I had no idea where the bus was heading. The morning of my birthday, Misty told me to wear something comfortable. So I walked out the front door in my comfortable clothes, and there on the curb was a literal, actual party bus. I couldn't see anyone inside; all I saw was this oversized black vehicle with music coming out. When I stepped inside the bus, I was met by thirty of our friends, who'd chipped in for this special surprise of food, drinks, laughter, and a hired chauffeur who drove us all the way to Chicago (about three hours away), where we could spend the whole afternoon at the art museum. I took only about a thousand pictures.

When we were done at the art museum, we drove over to the "Broadway in Chicago" area of the city and saw *West Side Story*, which was especially fun for me because back when I was in junior high and my brothers were in high school, we all danced in our hometown's version of the show.

They called my birthday celebration an "All Art Day for Arterburn," and I will long remember the great friends and sumptuous food, the astounding displays of color, form, and creativity. As a group, we sang all the best show tunes from *West Side Story* on the bus ride home.

On another birthday, we took all of our friends out for a Wine and Canvas evening. There was one dude in our group who was sure that this "painting thing" was fine for the rest of us, but he wasn't sure he wanted to participate. It took only a few minutes for him to catch the artsy bug, and the painting he created that night is still hanging in his home. You never know what sort of art you might enjoy until you throw caution aside and just playfully give it a try.

Decorating your home, taking your combined tastes and styles into consideration, is a way of daily surrounding yourself with beauty that makes you feel happy and uplifted, or calm and peaceful. And no other room in your home deserves more attention to beauty and detail than your bedroom. Because other people don't see the master bedroom, it's often the most neglected room in the house. But an act of love, a deposit into your passionate life together, is to create your own unique love nest and sanctuary of beauty in your bedroom.

- *TV.* I know many "love advisors" say that you shouldn't have a TV in the bedroom, that it's an excuse to avoid intimacy. But we love watching movies—like *An Affair to Remember* and *The Notebook*—that put us in the mood for romance. And we snuggle in bed while watching the occasional TV show. For us, it works. For other couples, not so much.
- *Bedding.* Having luxurious, comfy sheets, a great mattress (the thick foam toppers are awesome), a fluffy bedspread or duvet, and a soft throw blanket (heated, if you live where it is cold) for naps makes the bedroom a true retreat.
- *Ambience.* Think carefully about lighting. Lamps with dimmer switches are wonderful for bedside lighting to create a mood (and adjust to your most flattering light), and you can use them for soft light to read by, so as not to disturb a sleeping spouse. The kind of lamps you can just touch to turn on are noiseless as well, so you won't wake up your mate by turning them on or off. Window blinds and thin, light-colored curtains allow just enough morning light to cast a beautiful and sensual glow.
- *Fan or White Noise Machine.* Even in winter, one way to add white

noise to the room is to switch on a small fan that is turned away from your bed. This not only helps many people sleep better, it also adds another layer of soundproofing, which helps create the feeling of privacy.

- *Music.* Be sure to have a CD player or iPod docking station in your bedroom and/or master bath. Soft instrumental music is great when you are soaking in the tub, alone or together. It is also a good way to help you transition from the noise of the day into a more relaxed place, where you can snuggle or give each other a little massage or wind down with pillow talk.

BEAUTY IN LITERATURE AND THEATER

Couples who love to read always have something new to share with each other: a meaningful quote, a funny line, a scene of beauty, a fresh idea, a spiritual insight. Reading is one of life's daily, quiet pleasures that Misty and I share, enjoy, and bond over. We also love going to concerts and plays!

One of our best memories is of attending an outdoor concert in Hollywood with picnic basket in tow. It was one of Pavarotti's last performances. It transported us to another place, and the mood it inspired lingered, prompting conversations for days afterward. I mentioned earlier in this book that I was once a music major, and Misty, an incredible singer, grew up surrounded by musicians and music lovers, so perhaps it is of no surprise that our kids have soaked up a love for the arts and the stage. This past year, we got such a kick out of watching our son Solomon play the lead in *Aladdin.* And our two oldest boys brought tears to our eyes when we watched them each perform solos at different Christmas productions that sounded as though they came from angels in heaven. Oh, my. Do we ever love the arts!

Beyond books, concerts, and theater, our lives have been so enriched by all sorts of performing artists. Lately, our family has discovered and come to enjoy the hilarious and clean comedy of Brian

Regan. We love his funny video clips, so when we got tickets to see him in person, the whole family piled into the car with snickers and grins, anticipating the well-timed one-liners Brian would deliver as he poked fun at all of life.

Whether it's opera or bluegrass, critically acclaimed Broadway theater or down-home third-grade plays, serious drama or "laugh till you cry" comedy—the arts enhance our lives with beauty and passion.

One last note on appreciating beauty together. Sometimes this involves getting out of our comfort zone and engaging with what our partner finds beautiful. We go to her ballet, and even though men in tights is not our thing, we find ways to enjoy the experience, for her sake. We go to his rodeo and endure the *eau de manure*, dust, and noise because his eyes light up with excitement when the first cowboy on a bucking bronco rushes out of the pen. We see art through the other's eyes and at times stumble upon something beautiful we love to share together. Be open to seeing a wide variety of beautiful things through the eyes of your mate. You may be surprised by what you discover.

THE BEAUTY OF A WOMAN

You are altogether beautiful, my darling, beautiful in every way.

—SONG OF SOLOMON 4:7 NLT

Every woman needs to know that she is exquisite and exotic and chosen. This is core to her identity, the way she bears the image of God. Will you pursue me? Do you delight in me? Will you fight for me?

—JOHN ELDREDGE, *THE RANSOMED HEART*

Guys, look for the beauty in your wife as you would in a fine piece of art, because she is just that. Jean Anouilh, a French playwright, said,

"Things are beautiful if you love them." A woman who is well loved and cherished, no matter her age, radiates confident beauty. Have you heard the country song "You Look So Good in Love"? A woman in love has a glow about her that is unmistakable and alluring to the whole world. Misty with no makeup, her head on my pillow, the loveliness of her face, brings me to tears sometimes. Eleven years of marriage, and Misty still takes my breath away. I do my best to tell her these things when they rise up in my heart. Men, your words and actions have the power to make your wife literally beam with beauty, inside and out. If beauty is in the eye of the beholder, then husbands need to be sure they are good beholders, seeing their woman as God sees her: a magnificent, stunning creation.

Don't hold back when the thoughts and words of admiration well up in your heart. Tell your wife often that she is the "fairest of all" in your life. A woman who is treasured and regularly told she is lovely becomes ever more beautiful as the years pass by. And nothing will ignite her passion like being cherished as the one and only object of your deepest desire and affection. On the other hand, nothing will devastate a woman's self-esteem faster than being with a man who has a roving eye, who makes her feel that she is less attractive to him than other women.

John and Stasi Eldredge have written extensively about the core of a man's identity and a woman's identity in their bestselling books *Wild at Heart* and *Captivating*. In a nutshell, they believe men are like little boys constantly asking themselves, "Do I have what it takes?" Women, in contrast, are like little girls asking themselves, "Am I lovely?"

It is the privilege of a woman to answer her husband's unspoken question by assuring him that he is capable, by letting him know that she respects his ability to make his way through life's jungle, and by cheering him as he faces the daily battles at work. It is the honor of a man to assure his wife that she is lovely, alluring, beautiful in his eyes, and will always be the cherished treasure of his heart and affection. Of course, the roles are sometimes reversed and overlap: men also want to know that they are attractive to their wife, and love to hear compliments on their handsomeness or physique, and women love it when their man assures them that "they have what it takes" to accomplish a goal. But I think the Eldredges are mostly correct in their theory that the bottom-line desire of most males is to feel capable of fighting battles, slaying dragons, and rescuing their Beauty, in some form or another. And the key desire of a woman is to be swept into a grand romance, to be an equal partner in a great adventure, and to feel she is a true Beauty, worthy of being pursued and romanced.

No human can fulfill these core hungers quite like the love of God. God alone can answer many of the questions we have about our worth. As John Eldredge writes, "A woman in her glory, a woman of beauty, is a woman who is not striving to become beautiful or worthy or enough. She knows in her quiet center, where God dwells, that he finds her beautiful, has deemed her worthy, and in him, she is enough." A woman has to own her beauty, bestowed on her by Christ, who pursued her and died for her. A man has to believe he has what it takes because Christ, within, empowers him and makes him already accepted by the Father.

But a man and a woman, in relationship, have the privilege of echoing God's heart to each other as they speak his truth to one another every day. We are human manifestations of God's love, offering human approval and affection to each other. If done mutually, and done well, marriage is a magnificent healing, passionate force for good in the world. If done poorly, there are no words for the pain left in the wake of a mate's constant criticism or neglect.

I have observed that American husbands, too often, fall short in making their wife feel beautiful. There is a reason why single women from America and England flock to the Mediterranean when they need a shot of self-esteem. We have seen in a previous chapter that women of all ages and sizes seem to feel more admired and more beautiful in Spain than they would on Western soil. Why is that? And what can we guys learn from our Mediterranean brothers about how to make our woman feel gorgeous? Here are a few thoughts.

Eight Ways to Make Your Wife Feel
Beautiful, Mediterranean Style

1. *Straight up tell her she is beautiful: tell her often, with poetic enthusiasm!* Men from the Mediterranean are not shy about pouring on the compliments to women. They open their hearts and let the affirmations flow. "You are very beautiful." "What are you doing for the next hundred years?" "Your eyes are dazzling, like the sun." Or how about the line from the young Italian lover to the recently divorced middle-aged woman in *Under the Tuscan Sun*? "I am going to make love all over you." Think like an Italian stallion—just do it with your one and only!

2. *Use your facial expressions and gestures to convey approval.* A glance, a word, a pat, a raised eyebrow, a knowing smile, a wink. Be generous with the small, affectionate, nonsexual touches, as these feed a woman's need to be seen and loved, apart from always being a means to meet your sexual need.

3. *Appreciate all kinds of beauty.* Men from the Mediterranean tend to think that women as a whole, in all their variety, are simply beautiful. They love them at all ages, in all sizes and in all shapes. Many a middle-aged woman who felt invisible in her country has returned from Italy, Greece, or Spain feeling sexy, younger, and beautiful.

   One such woman from England, who described herself as ordinary and unnoticed in her home country, reported the story of being driven to the airport by a flirtatious Italian after spending some time in his country. She shared on a blog: "Well, to say I was bewitched and bedazzled is an understatement. By the time we got to Fiumicino, he could have said 'empty your wallet and give me all your credit cards' and I would have happily complied.

   "This may sound nuts but I came home a different person. I lost fifteen pounds and found the sexy woman that was buried and dormant underneath the grocery shopper/teacher/daughter/

bill payer/single mother. It's crazy but during that two-hour car trip, this young (fifteen years my junior) Italian man threw off my 'invisibility cloak,' and I am so grateful to him for that."

Imagine the power you have, as a husband, to help your wife feel sexy and young and beautiful with the words you shower upon her. Or a surprise passionate kiss out of nowhere. It wouldn't hurt most American men to learn the art of flirting and seduction from our Mediterranean brothers. Of course, unlike some Italian men, you would need to keep this skill directed at one woman, for a lifetime.

4. *Listen attentively, focus on her, compliment her thoughts, talents, wisdom, and creativity.* Mediterranean men tend to converse with women about ideas, philosophy, meaning, and culture. They enjoy hearing a woman's deeper thoughts and appreciate honest opinions. They give her their undivided attention and focus. In other words, they make her feel beautiful inside.

5. *Let her know you love her compassionate, intuitive heart.* The men of the Mediterranean wear their emotions on their sleeves, and they value a woman's emotions: tears of compassion, expressions of joy, tenderness toward children and the elderly and animals—all are noted and appreciated. Western men can have a way of making women feel weak when they feel and express deep emotion. Embrace and value your wife's gifts of intuition and emotional responses to life. God made her this way for a reason: you need her to balance and enrich your life.

6. *Let her into your heart and mind.* There are few things more captivating to a woman than a man being open and honest and vulnerable about his thoughts and feelings. Go for it—risk your heart with your wife when you sense her asking for you to share on a deeper level.

7. *Be a gentleman.* Men from the Mediterranean tend to be very gallant, especially when vying for a woman's attention. Open doors for your wife. Offer to carry in groceries and heavy

packages. Ask how you can help her. Guide her through crowds with your hand on the small of her back. Use good manners with her, show appreciation for all she does, and treat her like the queen of your heart, both at home and when you are out in public.

8. *Have some adventures together.* Plan and enjoy some adventures as a couple, whether it's snorkeling, hiking a mountain path, learning to kayak, taking a cooking lesson, or going to see a Broadway play. When you experience something new with one another, it is not only bonding but also exciting. It honors your wife by letting her know how much you enjoy her as a teammate and partner in exploring this beautiful world of ours.

———

A wise couple who want to remain passionately in love for a lifetime will proactively and frequently appreciate the beauty around them, whether that beauty is found in nature, in music, in art, or in each other's faces. One of the guests of San Salvatore, in the book *The Enchanted April,* said, "Beauty made you love, and love made you beautiful." Indeed, this is the funny thing about beauty. It inspires us to greater, more compassionate and generous feelings of love. And when we let love bloom and expand our hearts, we become more beautiful. One feeds the other in an endless circle of passion.

Thirteen Ways to Welcome Beauty into Your Life and Love

———

1. Go for a walk in a new and beautiful place, perhaps in a botanical garden or around a lake in an unfamiliar part of town.

2. Play romantic music as you cook and dine or in the car on road trips. Take CD players and CDs with you on getaways to hotels. Have a way to bring music into your master bath and bedroom.

3. Buy tickets to see a beautiful play, show, ballet, or opera together. Perhaps you can make it a surprise. Be willing to try something outside your comfort zone, especially if your spouse loves it.

4. Go together to an art museum, an aquarium, a museum of history, or a museum of nature.

5. Go to dinner somewhere that is not only known for its food but also has live music or a gorgeous view or both. Enjoy an unhurried evening, and prepare for the date by thinking of topics to discuss or questions to ask that get you talking about deeper subjects or new ideas and dreams.

6. Give your bedroom a romantic makeover. Talk about what elements would be most beautiful and sensual for you both, and come up with a plan to spruce up your love nest!

7. Write down twenty beautiful things you admire in your spouse. Either give them to each other in a card or share them one by one as the time seems right.

8. Find a poem, a song, or piece of art that reminds you of the beauty your mate brings to your life, and share it with them in an email, a card, or a text.

9. On a date night, make a list together of your favorite love songs, songs that remind you both of special moments with each other. Make a playlist for each of you to keep in the car.

10. Go to an art show, craft fair, or antique mall together. Give each other a budget and buy something you each find beautiful, to

display in your home or to wear. (Or put your money together and buy one bigger item.)

11. Plan a drive in the country on a beautiful day, stopping to eat at a quaint cafe or picnicking along the way.

12. Get near a beautiful body of water! Go to the ocean, a river, or a lake and spend the day there. You could ski, fish, snorkel, scuba dive, swim, or go out on a rented speedboat, pontoon boat, or jet skis. Or simply prop up two lounge chairs with snacks and cold drinks between you, a couple of books to browse, and enjoy the view.

13. Daydream and begin to plan for a trip to see something beautiful you've always wanted to see: the northern lights, Michelangelo's statue of David, a Tuscan vineyard, Stonehenge, the Hawaiian or Caribbean Islands.

CHAPTER 6

THE SECRET OF CREATIVITY

I have loved to the point of madness; that which is called
madness, that which to me, is the only sensible way to love.

—FRANCOISE SAGAN

A walk in Paris will provide lessons in history, beauty,
and in the point of Life.

—THOMAS JEFFERSON

Picasso, Vincent van Gogh, Monet, Salvador Dali.

Charles Dickens, F. Scott Fitzgerald, Ernest Hemingway, Gertrude Stein.

Chopin, Stravinsky, Josephine Baker, Cole Porter, George Gershwin.

Julia Childs, James Beard.

Christian Dior, Coco Chanel.

Isadora Duncan.

What do these names have in common? All of these people are artists—painters, writers, chefs, composers and singers, dancers, and fashion designers, from all over the world—who found exhilarating freedom, along with a rich social and cultural environment, in which to create in *La Ville Lumier*, the City of Light: Paris.

Blogger and writer Bryan Hutchinson expressed the effect of Paris on the creative soul: "When I walk the streets of Paris I feel as if the place is otherworldly, that God made this one place where artistic inspiration and creative energy meet to produce the divine."

The artistic tools might vary. They could be paintbrush or pen, chisel or ballet slippers, camera or chef's knife, musical instrument or operatic voice. But no one can deny that Paris has a centuries-long reputation for bringing out the artist's muse like few other places on earth can do.

A MOVEABLE FEAST

If you are lucky enough to have lived in Paris as a young man, then wherever you go for the rest of your life, it stays with you, for Paris is a moveable feast.

—ERNEST HEMINGWAY

If you have not seen the Woody Allen film *Moonlight in Paris*, well, you must. Rent it posthaste. This charming, romantic time-travel movie gives a delightful glimpse into many of the quirky, passionate artists of the Lost Generation who flocked to Paris between the two world wars in order to mingle with other artists, gather inspiration, create masterpieces, and live cheaply. The exchange rate was favorable for Americans in the 1920s, which helped them live on a meager and intermittent artist's income. Also, there was no Prohibition in Paris, and it is no secret that many of the expats there had a fondness for drinking.

The film shows that beyond producing novels, paintings, and musical scores, these artists-in-residence also fell in and out of love, with great regularity and plenty of passion.

Ernest Hemingway wrote about the magical, bohemian, creative years that served as the backdrop for *Moonlight in Paris* in his memoir *A Moveable Feast*. The writer tells of sitting in a quaint Parisian cafe one cold and rainy day to work on a novel. He starts out sipping a cafe au lait but soon graduates to a glass of rum. (It never took long, in Hemingway's memoirs, for him to graduate to alcohol. Usually after his morning coffee.) Before long, he spies a pretty, dark-haired girl sitting near a window.

"I looked at her and she disturbed me and made me very excited," he wrote. He wished for some personal interaction with the young lady, but he could see she was there waiting for someone else. At one point he looked up from his work, and moved again by her face and form, he penned one of his most famous lines: "I've seen you, beauty, and you belong to me now, whoever you are waiting for and if I never see you again, I thought. You belong to me and all Paris belongs to me and I belong to this notebook and this pencil."

After this declaration, Hemingway "went back to write and entered far into the story and was lost in it."[1]

It is fascinating to me to observe how, in this example, the act of writing in a small cafe along with the presence of a pretty lady prompted a bit of romantic daydreaming. And how the author's romantic imagination, in turn, inspired him to more creative work—to go deeper into the story he was writing.

Indeed, art and love often go together like cafe au lait and a fresh chocolate croissant. A sip of coffee calls for a bite of pastry. A bite of pastry begs for a sip of coffee. And so it goes with writing and romance, art and love.

I believe that creative energy is a much overlooked, and a powerful secret to arousing passion and romance between a man and a woman. Sensual feelings often appear when two people are in the creative zone, sharing the high of artistic energy. This is probably why workplace affairs (employees falling for each other while working on an exciting project) and affairs among artsy types (the choir director running off with the organist) are so common.

So why not harness the passionate energy that comes with creating art of any sort, then purposefully and proactively administer it, like an aphrodisiac, to our cherished monogamous relationships? Why leave this secret of sensuality to Mediterranean lovers, when we can access its power and spice up committed marriages?

CREATIVE FLOW, TOGETHER

When Hemingway said he entered the story and got lost in it, he was describing what Hungarian psychologist Mihaly Csikszentmihalyi (pronounced "Mee-hi Cheek-sent-me-high") calls the "state of flow."

Few things in life, Csikszentmihalyi believes, are as pleasurable and satisfying as entering "the flow," or "the zone," or what psychologist Abraham Maslow referred to as a "peak experience."

Contrary to what Americans often think, pure relaxation—chillin' out—doesn't really make us as happy as being in the state of flow, which requires concentrated effort. Csikszentmihalyi writes that the "best moments in our lives, are not the passive, receptive, relaxing times— although such experiences can also be enjoyable, if we have worked hard to attain them. The best moments usually occur when a person's body or mind is stretched to its limits in a voluntary effort to accomplish something difficult and worthwhile."[2]

He gives some examples of what flow looks like in everyday life. It could look like a child proudly and excitedly placing a block on a tower, higher than she's ever built it before, or a swimmer out to beat his own record, or a musician mastering a difficult musical passage. "For each person," he writes, "there are thousands of opportunities, challenges to expand ourselves."

There was a poignant time when I felt caught up in just such a state of flow. The middle brother in my family had been diagnosed with AIDS. This was in the late eighties. Tragically, the disease was so virulent that people who caught it did not have long to live. My brother Jerry led a troubled life. It was confused, complex, duplicitous. Somehow he was able to keep his secret from me until I was twenty-six years old. He'd been molested by a preacher's son when he was young and had never shared this with my parents. And now he was down to ninety pounds and trying to figure out how to tell Mom and Dad that he was gay and dying. He felt he had a story to tell that he hoped would prevent others from molestation and its effects.

I have to say, this was a horrific tragedy that I never saw coming. Not to our Southern Baptist family. And certainly not to Jerry. He was an architect, and his life appeared to be as well-planned as the blueprint of a high-rise. He and I had pulled our money together to buy a boat that we loved taking out on Lake Conroe, near our hometown in Texas. Later, he and I would go in together to buy an oceangoing boat in Newport Beach, California. So many great memories out on the water with my brother! He was classy and movie star handsome.

In the middle of the worst of his misery and emotional turmoil, he asked me to write down his story in a book that would eventually be published and titled *How Will I Tell My Mother?* Spurred on by love for my brother, by the limited time to honor his wishes, I wrote, as we say in Texas, like a house afire. Sentence after sentence poured out of my heart; pages of stories flowed like a river out of my computer's printer. When I was finished, I gathered up the pages and took them to read aloud to my brother as he lay in his bed. The book was a true reflection of my brother—creative, full of life and humor, sadness and confusion, desire for meaning and love for God. He wept as I read his life back to him, and there were times when I had to pause to catch the lump in my throat. He loved it. And I loved him loving it. I cannot express what it meant to me that God allowed me to use my gifts of listening, capturing stories in my mind, and telling them again on paper to bring comfort and joy to my big brother in his last hours on earth.

You never know when or how God may use your creative talents to bless someone in ways you never dreamed about. I believe that one way the Holy Spirit directs us to our God-given talents that will bless the world is by getting us caught up in this state of flow. I am sure many of you reading this remember a time when you were working on a creative project that had special meaning or purpose or value to you. Time ceased to exist; you felt almost as if you were just a reed, a conduit of

God's creativity, allowing his Spirit to simply flow through you. As if the Creator of the universe wanted you to know the joy of creating as well. How do you know if you are in the flow? You're deeply immersed in what you are doing, and time seems to fly. You feel clearheaded: you know what you need to do to finish the task ahead, and you believe you have the skill set needed to accomplish it. You aren't self-conscious, and worries drift away because of the concentration needed and the pleasure involved in the task.

Most of us can recall times when we have, individually, been caught up in creative flow. But have you and your mate ever experienced working *together*—on anything creative—and found yourself moving into a zone where everything feels seamless, as if you don't have to use words, because the other simply gets what you are doing, almost reading your mind? Where time seems to disappear because you are so focused on what the two of you are creating? The feeling of energetic joy that comes out of these shared moments can be profoundly bonding and romantic.

You can experience flow as a couple by working on a shared activity (more practical ideas for this to come) or by being together while you are in the same outdoor space or indoor room, caught up in something you both love to do. The more creative, the better!

I have friends, passionately and happily married, both in the professional writing industry. Sometimes they work on the same book project—brainstorming outlines or titles, with ideas bursting between them like popcorn. "We work together like a well-oiled machine at these times, lost in our own creative bubble," the wife shared.

Her husband agreed. "It's a natural high, no doubt. And there's often sexy sparks flying back and forth when we are in this zone. The more creative we get, as the project unfolds, the more we tend to flirt. It makes my workday feel much more like play."

However, most of the time, this literary couple is writing on laptops, in the same room together but not talking. Still, they experience a sort of "quiet, happy, connected flow" between them—even while working on separate projects.

Misty and I get this, especially now. Writing this book, a true heart-project for us, has opened new layers of passion. We are pulled together, caught up in like-minded flow. Things that might have normally irritated us don't seem to bother us while we're focused on writing a book that we hope will help other couples catch the fire of passion! We have laughed and cried as we've reminisced about our marriage and searched for the secrets that led us from frustration to passion. This creative, meaningful project has brought us closer to one another than we ever dreamed it would when we first brainstormed the concept. I think part of the reason for this is that we've been able to use our individual writing gifts as a team, in tandem, in ways we never have before. As a result, we are experiencing creative flow together. And it has definitely increased the passion factor in our days. There has been a lot of fun, private connecting between the lines that ended up in this book.

This outcome for us has made me think that a fun project for every couple would be to write your love story together sometime. Talk about and write down the highlights of your unique, personal romance—the moments in your relationship when you experienced a surge of love and passion that you never want to forget. You may be surprised, as we've been, to find yourselves reliving the highlights of love in a walk down memory lane, feeling emotions that arise, overflow into the present, and overwhelm you all over again.

Whether you and your spouse are working side by side on a shared creative project or working in close proximity on separate endeavors that bring you both into a state of flow, the experience of getting lost in time together can be bonding, stimulating, and passion inspiring.

BONDING THROUGH SELF-EXPANDING ACTIVITIES

Let's face it: boredom is the enemy of passion. And yet living together, especially while raising a family, requires a lot of routine, ritual, and stability. What to do?

Begin by simply being aware that keeping passion alive means purposefully, proactively reserving time for what some psychologists call "self-expanding" activities. Research suggests that couples who feel most intensely in love are the ones who not only have strong physical chemistry and emotional attraction but also regularly participate in new activities together. If these activities involve even a small risk or challenge, all the better. Because when you accomplish a challenge as a couple or try something new (as easy as going to a restaurant you've never been to before), you've expanded your feeling of conquering new territory together, and this causes a romantic rush.

"Novel and arousing activities are, well, arousing, which people can misattribute as attraction to their partner, reigniting that initial spark," writes psychologist and social researcher Amie Gordon.[3]

Psychologist and relationship researcher Arthur Aron collaborated on a 2012 study to discover why some couples stayed wildly passionate about each other after many years of marriage.[4] The researchers found that couples who feel passionate about one another experience regular strong doses of dopamine, a neurotransmitter that makes us feel energetic pleasure. One important way couples trigger the release of dopamine in each other is by spending time together in new and challenging activities. Studies found this was especially true for active men, who tend to bond more deeply over going kayaking together, perhaps, than a long conversation "about the relationship" over afternoon tea.

According to Aron's research, novelty is a key ingredient in a passionate long-term relationship. This doesn't mean you give up your favorite fun rituals together, but you do want to make an effort to incorporate some new and different activities into the mix. This could be anything from taking a painting or cooking class as a couple or going for a walk in a new neighborhood to riskier adventures like skydiving or rock climbing. It depends on the couple's personality and preferences. Just pick something you haven't done together before (or recently) that you'd both like to try (or experience again).

Though new and challenging activities produce dopamine that creates feelings of exhilaration and passion, just spending time with one another on any creative project—say, sprucing up the basement or gardening—is also very bonding for couples, evoking other pleasurable neurotransmitters such as serotonin and oxytocin. Again, mix it up! Enjoy the familiar creative activities together, but push yourselves now and then to try an activity you've never engaged in before.

As mentioned earlier, the best way for many males to feel close to their spouse is to work on a project or task together. This is one reason why I encourage women to combine their need for communication with some sort of physical activity, especially if their husband has a hard time sitting still. Chat with him while he's polishing the car, or go for a walk as you talk. You'll find that many men, especially those with ADHD tendencies, focus more and hear you better if they can also walk, row, fish, or fiddle with something—any repetitive activity that keeps their body moving so their mind can better focus.

MAKING YOUR OWN SUNSHINE

There is no getting around it: at some point, each person in a partnership has to take responsibility for becoming happier and more passionate individuals. A 2012 Stony Brook University study discovered that "individuals who exhibit excitement for all of life" were more likely to enjoy healthy and long-lasting romance.[5]

"People who approach their daily lives with zest and strong emotion seem to carry these intense feelings over to their love life as well," wrote Susan Krauss Whitbourne in *Psychology Today*. "If you want your relationship to have passion, put that emotional energy to work in your hobbies, interests, and even your political activities."[6]

Though all couples need commitment, safety, and stability, if this is all a marriage has going for it, the result can start to look like neediness or caretaking or boredom. Not exactly the sexiest things in the world.

When your partner gets a chance, however, to observe you doing something you're passionate about, something that requires a little courage, something in which your talents shine, it allows them a brief shift in perspective. When we discover some new talent or skill in our partner, it often increases feelings of surprise, passion, and desire.

The musical apple did not fall far from her father's tree, so it was no surprise to me to learn that Misty has a great voice. But I'd just caught little bits of her singing here and there. Imagine my surprise when I heard her sing her first solo in church and realized, "Oh, my goodness. My wife could have been a recording artist." She sang in a style I'd never heard before and haven't heard since—a little southern gospel, a little contemporary country, a little of Misty's own unique style.

I once captured a photo of Misty singing that still moves me when I walk by it. Her eyes are shut, her mouth is open, as splendorous words of praise are drifting upward. And she isn't alone in the picture; our yet-to-be-born daughter, Amelia Pearl Arterburn, is curled up inside Misty's pregnant belly. I honestly don't know how I was able to take that picture in that moment, because I was so full of joy, so grateful for the miracle of a precious wife and the impending birth of my daughter, so moved by Misty's voice giving praise to the Giver of these unspeakable gifts, that I was a mess of tears.

Don't let yourself become apathetic or dull. Keep your creative and curious spirit alive by pushing yourself to try some new adventures or learn some new skills. There is nothing more attractive to the opposite sex than a happy person in love with life, who is interested in discovering new ideas, learning new information, and trying new activities. So take ownership of your own zest for life, your *joie de vivre*.

After our son Solomon was born in 2006 and started toddling and talking, the oddest thing happened to me. I took up colored pencils and started to draw. Solomon, as a preschooler, responded to my drawings as if I were his personal Van Gogh. So I started a tradition of creating fun pictures and word art with colored pencils when I traveled, to let my family know I was thinking of them. Elmo and Mickey Mouse were among the subjects of my first, highly praised portraits.

Little did I know then that someday art journaling, drawing your prayers, and adult coloring books would become all the rage. I was drawing and coloring long before it became a fad! I was doodling before doodling was cool.

One day I was doing a radio show with Dr. Sheri Keffer, a therapist with NewLife. While we talked on air, I was doodling. I had taken my daughter's name—Amelia Pearl—and created a monogram of her initials, in sort of a *Frozen* meets *Cinderella* meets *Peppa Pig* style. Dr. Keffer asked if others had accused me of not paying attention to them, or to a sermon or a class (or a live radio show), when they saw me drawing. "All the time," I said. "But I can't seem to stay still and focus *unless* my hands are busy!" She said, "Steve, with people who have ADHD, drawing and doodling actually helps them listen better and helps them stay engaged and on topic. When you draw, it is a way to flip the 'on switch' in your brain. Then you are actually more alert and stay more focused on the topic at hand."

Remember how I used to call my paternal grandfather Dad Art—a nickname for Arterburn? Misty has, over the past two years, begun calling me Art. From the garage on her way to the grocery store, she will call out, "Hey, Art! Are we out of bread?" Ask me how much I love this. It has come to me late in life, but I do like to think of myself as an artist of sorts now. And after hearing Dr. Keffer's explanation, I realize I am my own art therapist. Misty's term of endearment for me, connecting me to my grandfather and validating the artist she sees in me, touches my soul intimately, in a way that's hard to describe. All I can say is, I am grateful.

Now that doodling and coloring is cool for adults to do, thousands of right-brained creative types, or those of us with ADHD, are suddenly being praised for our creativity and artistic style. If only this had been true when I was a kid. I am just glad that so many adults are realizing that drawing, doodling, coloring, and painting relaxes the mind. It's what psychiatrists call a "centering activity," and it gives the amygdala, the part of the brain associated with anxiety and fear, a much-needed rest.

Not long ago, Misty came to me and said, "Steve, I have an idea." Since I *love* new ideas, I was all ears. She had a few close friends who had all been through some sort of major trauma, and by working the twelve steps together, going to recovery meetings, these women had come out the other side stronger, more fulfilled, and more real. Misty wanted to start a website and Facebook page called Recovery Girls to motivate women—with a wide variety of issues—to get into recovery and experience freedom.

I told my wife she was brilliant. This was a fabulous idea! Her eyes lit up with excitement, and it was a lot of fun to watch her normal routine disintegrate as she—fueled by surges of fresh ideas and caught up in the flow—poured hours into creating a website, making videos, holding photo shoots, consultations, and meetings. The passion beneath this frenzy of activity was Misty's deep desire to provide hope for struggling women who needed a dab of strength and a pinch of guidance from sisters who understood their daily battles.

The benefit for me? There's no greater joy than seeing my wife soar! When she is happy, when she is doing what she feels called and gifted to do, I fall in love with new sides of her that I never realized existed before.

Two people in love with life and with each other are bound to enjoy a long and passionate relationship. So get those creative juices flowing, get in touch with your inner artist, and have fun! Then take it one step farther, and ask God how he might use your creative talents to bless someone else in a meaningful way. Whether you serve together as a couple in some ministry or take turns cheering and supporting each other, there's nothing quite like the passion that flows from being a vessel of blessing to the world.

Thirteen Ways to Get Creative with Your Lover

1. Get away together to an energizing, culturally rich city. Of Paris, James Joyce wrote, "No other city is quite like it. I wake early, often at 5 o'clock, and start writing at once." Have you noticed

that some cities seem to have an electrical current of energy about them? Besides Paris, most people feel this energy when they are in big cities like New York or Chicago. And many creative types thrive there. Most of us live near enough to a big city that we can drive to its cultural center and spend a day walking through art museums, nature museums, or history museums, or people-watch at a sidewalk cafe or take in a live concert or play or musical. So plan a day in the city together, absorbing its culture, then notice how the energy of the artists affects you. You may very well find yourselves with fresh motivation to try your hand at new creative projects or some sort of art.

2. Go to an inspirational setting. To balance the cultural energy in the city, head out to places that are more serene, laid back, and beautiful and allow you space to think and create. Big cities often inspire us to create. But most of us need serenity and quiet—a beach, a camping spot, a coffee shop—to take the next step and begin creating. These places give us room to write, paint, draw, or brainstorm new ideas.

3. Shake it up! Think about something you already enjoy doing regularly together—say, walking around your neighborhood or browsing a local bookstore. And ponder how you can shake it up a bit. Drive to a new neighborhood and walk—or bike or skate—around it. Do a little research and explore a new bookstore in another part of town; combine your visit there with going for dessert and coffee at a French cafe you've never tried before. Sometimes it is easier to start being more adventurous by springboarding off the activities you know and enjoy.

4. Paint together. Go to one of the popular "canvas and cocktail" events in your town. They are springing up everywhere (check the internet for discounts, such as Groupons), and they are a

great, easy, fun way to enjoy a night out in which you and your spouse are participants in the creative arts rather than just spectators.

5. Take classes together. Research community education classes in your area. These affordable classes, typically offered at a local community college on evenings and weekends, are a rich resource for creative date nights. They cover a wide array of subjects, and they vary in length. Some are one-night seminars; others are six-week (one night a week) courses. There is something for everyone, and you will be amazed at all the great things you can learn to do—from "How to Make Sushi on a Shoestring" to "How to Paint Like Monet" to "How to Be a Clown for Fun and Profit." Pick a class that sounds fun and interesting to both of you and sign up!

6. Create your own romantic cards. Skip the pricey stuff and connect with your inner child: spend a little time with paper, scissors, glue, markers, lace, buttons, and stickers, and create a card for your beloved that comes from your heart, either for Valentine's Day or just because. You can make a "dry-erase board" out of a solid piece of colored paper—with the words "I Love You Because . . ." written at the top—tucked into a pretty glass picture frame. Keep it somewhere special, all year long, and take turns writing impromptu love notes to each other with a dry-erase marker (attach it to the frame) as the mood hits.

7. Color your heart out. At this writing, adult coloring books are all the rage! Along with these fill-in-the-blank coloring pages, there are books that inspire you to draw your prayers or illustrate Scripture verses. This is a wonderful way for creative types to connect with their inner artist while also connecting with God and spiritual meaning.

8. Play your own kind of music. If you've always wanted to learn how to play an instrument, what is stopping you from taking lessons? Go for it! Or maybe you used to play the sax back in high school, but it is now gathering dust in the attic. Go get it, clean it up, and give it a go. Gather the family around a campfire for impromptu, home-style sing-alongs. (You can create campfire ambiance around a back patio fire pit or indoor fireplace or even a grouping of candles on a coffee table.) If nobody in your family plays an instrument, you can hand out a tambourine or a kazoo to a couple of the kids. Sing in the car, dance in the kitchen, grab your guitar and serenade whoever is cooking dinner. Let music become a natural part of your life.

9. Take a pottery class. One- or two-hour classes that cater to beginners who want to try their hand at pottery are popping up in most towns. Who knows? You two might fall in love with the medium of clay—and end up recreating the potter's wheel love scene that Demi Moore and Patrick Swayze made famous in the movie *Ghost*.

10. Pursue whatever talent God has given you. Have you always wanted to act? Try out for a part in the local community theater. Do you have a beautiful voice that you aren't using to bless others? Join a choir or an ensemble. Give yourself permission to develop your God-given talents, individually, to keep your creative spirit alive. Support each other in these pursuits, and sit in the front row—literally and figuratively—cheering and clapping and encouraging one another in using your gifts and talents.

11. Pass along your talents. There is so much meaning in teaching your children or grandkids to play an instrument or showing them how to paint with watercolors or make a birdhouse or

dance an Irish jig. A friend of mine told me, "When I was in junior high, our youth director offered to give group guitar lessons to all the kids in our small youth group. I am fifty-six now, and to this day, I think of the gift he gave me when I strum the guitar and sing with my grandkids." Whatever your talent—decorating cakes or building a treehouse—share it with others.

12. Be each other's number one fan. When you watch your mate perform any kind of creative artwork, be sure to tell them how proud you are of their gifts and the courage they've shown in using those talents. Assure them of how happy it makes you to see them in their creative element, in the flow, in their zone. This can be as simple as saying something like, "I loved watching you teach our daughter how to sew today. You were so patient and encouraging. You are passing down a legacy of creativity!" Or, "I am so proud of the landscaping you've done in the backyard. I sit out there in the mornings with my coffee and just soak up the beauty you helped create."

13. Plan an "adventure of the month" together. It doesn't matter what it is; just try something new, something that is at least a little challenging. It should be more active than passive. (For example, take a cooking class rather than eating at a new restaurant.) Push yourselves a bit out of your comfort zone on this one. Go big. Think outside the box!

CHAPTER 7

THE SECRET OF HEALTH
AND LONGEVITY

I gave you life so that you could live it!

—MARIA PORTOKALOS, *MY BIG FAT GREEK WEDDING*

———

I recently hit another milestone birthday, bringing me much closer to the age when I can say whatever I want and be instantly forgiven.

I do not have the luxury of retiring from either work or physical activity at my age, thanks to the young family I am in the midst of raising. Needless to say, my interest in staying young at heart and fit in body is at an all-time high. I not only want to be around to see my little ones graduate from college, marry, and have children of their own; I want to have most of my marbles when it happens. I want to join my kids in energetic outings when they are young adults, camping with their little families; I want to drive a boat and pull everyone on water skis around a lake, the way my father used to pull his grandkids; I want to vacation with everyone as a clan, living to the fullest in the best years of life. At the very least, I want to walk my daughter down the aisle without a cane. You've probably guessed by now that I would also love to enjoy many more second honeymoons with Misty.

The benefit of having little kids is that because I am always surrounded by youthful energy, their youthful spirits and attitudes are contagious. The downside of this is that if I allowed myself to think like an elderly person, it could be really depressing to be the old rooster in a coop of spring chickens. Thankfully, even before I married Misty and we had babies together, I always felt younger (and often more immature) than my actual age. Chalk it up to late blooming or general hardheadedness; it took me a good while to grow up, find my way to God, and get my act together.

Even so, there are a few signs of aging I can't ignore. A couple years ago, I performed an age-inappropriate stunt on a skateboard. The result of that little demonstration was a broken tibia, a torn meniscus, and the dreaded shredded ACL. A man of tact, my surgeon never hinted that I might try a different way of showing my kids that their ol' Dad still had it. In recent months, I've been recovering from a second knee surgery. This time, my surgeon was a little more to the point: "Arterburn, you might want to take it easy on activities that might blow out your knees." He did not add, "Because, aren't you getting a little old for this stuff?" Still, I knew it was implied. So I have a renewed and keen interest in stories about anyone over age fifty who defies the normal aging decline and lives with passion, energy, movement, and adventure. Especially when two people do so as a couple, together.

Though my life circumstances may not be the norm, I know I am not alone in my desire to stay as virile and healthy as I can until the good Lord calls me home. Baby boomers, as a whole, have refused to go gently into that geriatric good night, and Generation X has embraced the anti-aging trend with just as much vigor. So I think most readers may find the following story as fascinating and inspiring as I did.

THE ISLE OF ETERNAL YOUTH[1]

For I realize today that it is a mortal sin to violate the
great laws of nature. We should not hurry, we should

not be impatient, but we should confidently obey the
eternal rhythm.

—NIKOS KAZANTZAKIS, *ZORBA THE GREEK*

Ikaria, Greece, is a place where people are far more likely to become centenarians—and happy, healthy, physically and sexually active ones at that. One of the more fascinating personal stories of longevity and health is featured in the second edition of the book *The Blue Zones* by Dan Buettner. While Buettner was interviewing a 102-year-old Ikarian woman about her secret to longevity, she told him, "We just forget to die." This phrase caught on, and Ikaria was dubbed the Island Where People Forget to Die.[2]

Buettner tells of a man named Stamitis Moraitia, Greek by birth, who came to America as a war veteran in 1943. He and his wife, Elpniki, were living in Florida in 1976 when he fell ill. Ten doctors confirmed his diagnosis of lung cancer, giving him nine months to live. He was in his mid-sixties. He decided to return to his native home, the sunny, hilly island of Ikaria, about one hundred square miles in size, to live out the remainder of his days. In his ancestral land, he could be buried more cheaply, in a family cemetery overlooking the Aegean Sea. Once back in the country of his youth, he and Elpniki moved in with his elderly parents, who lived in a small, whitewashed home on two hilly acres of vineyards.

Buettner writes, "At first, Moraitia spent his days in bed. On Sunday mornings, he hobbled up the hill to a tiny Greek Orthodox chapel, where his grandfather once served as a priest. When his childhood friends started showing up every afternoon, they'd talk for hours, an activity that invariably involved a bottle or two of locally produced wine."[3] The dying man thought that he might as well spend his last days being happy. However, something odd began to happen. Stamitis Moraitia began to feel stronger. He planted a garden, and as he worked in the sunshine, he breathed lots of fresh ocean air into his diseased lungs.

Before long, Stamitis found himself easing into the typical Ikarian routine: waking when he felt like it, working the vineyards, napping in the afternoon. In the evenings, he often walked to join his friends at the local tavern, where he played dominoes, sometimes until after midnight. Interestingly, his health continued to improve, and he was able to build a couple of rooms onto his parents' home so his adult children, living in America, could come visit. He also worked the family vineyard until it yielded four hundred gallons of wine per year. He never went through chemotherapy, took drugs, or sought treatment of any sort. All he did was return home to Ikaria and live the simple, active, social life he'd known as a boy. When he did so, his body forgot it had cancer, forgot to be sick, forgot to die. One decade after another, he thrived.

Moraitia lived a long, happy, cancer-free life until he passed away in his own home in 2013, at the age of 98 (though he said he was actually 102, believing the records of his birth to have been inaccurate). He outlived his wife by more than a decade (she passed away at age 85). In an interesting side note, Stamitis Moraitia returned to America some twenty-five years after he left, to see if he could find the doctors who diagnosed him with lung cancer and learn exactly what occurred that healed him. But he could not follow through on his mission, for all his doctors were dead by then.

Though Stamitis's story of a near-miraculous recovery from malignant cancer may be unusual, the good health, vitality, and longevity of the Ikarians is typical. Ikaria is unique among the Greek Isles, in that it is fairly isolated from the modern world. These healthy islanders live ten hours by boat from the metropolis of Athens, where the national rate of obesity has soared since its introduction to Western habits of consumerism and eating fast food. Ikarians, however, are still two and a half times as likely to reach age ninety as are Americans, and the men are nearly four times as likely to reach ninety as are men in the United States. The ten thousand residents of Ikaria experience about a quarter of our rate of dementia, and in spite of the high rate of unemployment and other challenges, they experience significantly less depression than do Americans.

So what are Ikarians doing that we Westerners are not, to yield such long, happy, vital lives? Researchers are finding that there isn't one isolated factor that leads to vitality and longevity. As Dan Buettner said, "There is no silver bullet." What he found in his research on the longest-lived, healthiest people in the world was that a number of healthy habits work in tandem—more like "silver buckshot"—to yield ideal conditions for long, passionate, and contented lives.[4]

Interestingly, Greece, as a country, also has the lowest divorce rate in Europe, and the most active sex life among elderly couples, consistently a sign of marital satisfaction in long-term marriages. I couldn't help but be curious about the habits of the Greeks and the Ikarians, since this island boasts some of the healthiest, happiest, sexiest elders on the planet.

In case you are curious as well, here are some of the habits of these hearty, happy islanders.

1. Ikarians stay up very late and sleep until they wake naturally, without an alarm.
2. They always take a nap in the afternoon.
3. They don't care much about the clock; they are not schedule- or time-oriented.
4. They drink what they call "mountain tea," made from local herbs and served as an evening cocktail. The tea is considered a tonic for good health. It has strong antioxidant properties, and properties that keep blood pressure naturally and gently lowered.
5. The typical daily routine for Ikarians is to wake naturally and slowly, work in the garden or vineyards or tending goats, then have a late lunch, followed by a nap. At sunset they visit with friends, often over wine. (Good news for those who enjoy an afternoon snooze: people who nap three times a week are found to have 37 percent fewer heart troubles than those who don't nap.)
6. Like people in other Mediterranean countries, Ikarians eat very little meat and sugar and lots of legumes, vegetables, and olive oil. In addition, their diet is rich in goat's milk, locally grown

organic red wine (two to four cups a day), their mountain tea, strong Greek coffee (two to three cups a day), local fresh honey, and heavy, wholegrain sourdough bread. Meals are often beans, potatoes, greens, and seasonal vegetables from their garden. Meat is rarely eaten, but when it is consumed, it is typically fish, goat, or pork.

Doctors from the University of Athens Medical School found that goat's milk contained tryptophan, which produces serotonin, a hormone that gives people a general feeling of contentment and happiness. Also, goat's milk is more easily digestible than cow's milk. There are more than 150 types of edible island greens that have ten times as many antioxidants as red wine. Wine—in moderation—prompts the body to absorb more disease- and cancer-fighting flavonoids, a type of antioxidant. Sourdough bread, made of whole grains, can reduce a meal's glycemic load. And all their produce is chemical- and pesticide-free.

7. In a study of older Ikarian men (between ages sixty-five and one hundred), 80 percent claimed to have sex regularly. A quarter of that group said they were doing so with "good duration" and "achievement."[5] Greeks, as a nation, also have sex with more frequency than do people in most other countries in the world, averaging three times a week. Zorba the Greek said, "If a woman sleeps alone it puts a shame on all men. God has a very big heart, but there is one sin he will not forgive. If a woman calls a man to her bed and he will not go."

To Greeks, sex is a gift, and one not to be ignored! According to a survey, 80 percent of Greeks believe that having sex is very important, as opposed to, say, citizens of Thailand, where only 38 percent believe that sex is important. In addition, lovemaking lasts longer among Greeks than in most of the world, averaging 22.3 minutes.[6]

8. Besides eating more naturally and healthfully than Americans, the Greeks slow down to thoroughly relax and enjoy their

meals. They rarely dine alone, preferring the company of family and friends. Food is enjoyed with a heavy side of conversation. When they converse, other than local gossip, they love discussing loftier subjects such as philosophy and the meaning of life—as did their Greek ancestors. Socrates, that ancient wise Greek, said, "Strong minds discuss ideas, average minds discuss events, weak minds discuss people."

9. Although unemployment is high—perhaps as high as 40 percent—Greeks work very hard, long hours on the chores of survival. They may start their workday late (typically not until 11:00 a.m.), but many of its citizens also work late into the night. Almost everyone has gardens and raises either goats or pigs. In addition, the Ikarians often work several part-time, odd, or seasonal jobs as the opportunity arises.

10. Though not rich in money, Ikarians are rich in community, laughter, friends, and family. They may not have expendable income for luxuries, but their self-sufficiency means there is always fresh, natural food on the table. Their basic needs are few, and they can meet these needs without a lot of money.

11. The elderly of the island attribute their longevity to clean air and wine. Although there is pollution around the mainland, the island of Ikaria is more isolated, so the air there has remained pure and clean. They drink two to four glasses a day of the locally produced, pesticide-free wine.

12. Besides gardening and caring for mountain goats, a typical day involves walking up twenty hills. The main mode of transportation from house to work and entertainment is walking. And evenings are often filled with dancing. For Ikarians of all ages, exercise is a natural part of life—their transportation, their work, their entertainment.

13. The culture has great respect for the elderly, and people feel a sense of purpose to their lives, all of their lives.

14. Greek Orthodox religion is woven into their daily experience,

which gives their lives a sense of purpose, stability, community, belonging, and compassion. For the many religious and cultural holidays, people pool their money and buy food and wine. If there is money left over, they give it to the poor. On Sunday they attend church, and they fast before Orthodox feast days. "Even if you're antisocial, you'll never be entirely alone," writes Buettner. "Your neighbors will cajole you out of your house for the village festival to eat your portion of goat meat."

15. At the beginning of the movie *My Big Fat Greek Wedding*, the female lead, Toula, tries to explain to her new boyfriend, Ian, what it is like to belong to a Greek family. "My whole family is big and loud. And everybody is in each other's lives and business. All the time! Like, you never just have a minute alone, just to think, 'cause we're always together, just eating, eating, eating! The only other people we know are Greeks, 'cause Greeks marry Greeks to breed more Greeks, to be loud breeding Greek eaters."

This hilarious movie is amazingly accurate in the way it portrays the Greek mindset. They don't think in terms of "me" as much as "us" or "we." There is no Greek word for privacy. This lack of privacy can be frustrating at times, but it also keeps bad behavior in check, as everyone knows what everyone else is doing. There's low crime here, not because of good policing but because people do not want to bring shame to their family. And as annoying as it may sometimes be, the sense of belonging is one of the basic human needs. And boy, do Greeks feel that they are needed, that there is a welcoming place for them, that they belong to family and the community. This is great fodder for longevity.

At the end of *My Big Fat Greek Wedding*, Toula concludes, "My family is big and loud but they're my family. We fight and we laugh and yes, we roast lamb on a spit in the front yard. And wherever I go, whatever I do, they will always be there."

EXERCISING FOR HEALTH, ENERGY, AND PASSIONATE LIVING

No man has the right to be an amateur in the matter of physical training. It is a shame for a man to grow old without seeing the beauty and strength of which his body is capable.

—SOCRATES

Greece is one of only two European countries to be ranked among the top ten most physically active nations in the world. (The Netherlands, that country of endless bicycles, is the other. However, the Greeks are even more active than the biking Netherlanders.)[7] Life expectancy in Greece is 81.4 years.[8] This is among the highest in the world.

Along with diet and a sense of belonging and purpose, another reason why many Europeans (and particularly Mediterraneans) are more fit than Americans is that they live where exercise is a natural part of getting around town. They don't have to carve out time to go to the gym, because life itself—going to and fro—has built-in workouts.

In a study of seventeen industrialized countries, Americans had the highest rate of obesity and were least likely to walk, cycle, or take mass transit. Europeans, on the other hand, walked three times as far and cycled five times as far as Americans, in most part because their cities are more compact and conducive to getting around via active means.

Researchers found that Europeans, on average, walk 237 miles and cycle 116 miles per year; U.S. residents walk 87 miles and bike 24 miles. This means that Europeans naturally burn off five to nine pounds of fat annually, compared with only two pounds for Americans.[9]

Americans were not always as unfit as they are today. With the advent of fast food and drive-through restaurants in Western culture, our access to calories has increased. And as the calories have increased, we've decreased the amount of physical activity in our lives. In 1970, about 40 percent of all children in the U.S. walked to school; now fewer than 12 percent do. Our grandparents, without exercising, burned up about five times as many calories a day in physical activity as we do. Unlike my father and grandfather, I didn't have to trudge five miles through snow to school and back. I was driven to school. However, I did walk home, and it *was* more than a mile, and I had to cross a major thoroughfare in the heat and humidity of Bryan, Texas. Okay, maybe it wasn't as bad as my father and his father had it, but it was a far cry from the ten steps to the school bus my kids take.

I am aware, however, that my kids are going to catch a lot more from observing their dad prioritize fitness than from my lecturing them about how hard I had it when I was their age. So they see an active man who is up and exercising even though there are mornings when this feels like an almost impossible feat. They have come to know that it is in movement that we bring life back into our bodies, sustain its health, and prolong its vitality. (Rather than the coffin-preparatory pose most assume on the couch in front of the TV.) Today's kids are seldom seen without some kind of screen: iPhone, laptop, Game Boy, iPad, TV, and on it goes. Rather than nag at my kids to turn off the technology, I try to make it fun to be active, and invite them to go on a bike ride or to throw around a ball or to take a hike somewhere special.

Misty and I both lead naturally active lives, and we are betting on this to help keep us young and give us the energy needed to be fully available to our kids, our work, and each other for a lifetime. Everyone in our family has a bicycle, and we all ride together on some fun shorter rides. Misty and I also get away and take longer rides through the corn-fields about a minute from our house. Misty does CrossFit, and I do the rowing machine and weight lifting. We love the chance to get outside to play sports and take long walks in the woods, and when we have the opportunity, we love to ride horses. And you've already read about our favorite indoor exercise: dancing!

EXERCISE AS THE FOUNTAIN OF YOUTH

Because Greece is the birthplace of the Olympic Games, the Greek government takes physical activity to heart. From a young age, children are geared toward sports. Sadly, in every place that becomes more Westernized with the influx of media, consumerism, and fast food, the fitness of the area goes down and obesity rises.

Dr. Daniel Amen, one of the leading experts in America on the subject of brain health and aging, writes, "Physical exercise is truly the fountain of youth and it is critical for keeping your brain vibrant and young." Walking five days a week for just thirty minutes a day can slow dementia and even stop it in its tracks. Some studies indicate that walking thirty minutes a day can prevent Alzheimer's from developing, even if you are genetically predisposed for it.[10]

Dr. Amen has become a good friend to me and my brain, after he discovered I had a traumatic brain injury that showed up in the spec scans he recently took. Once he discovered the problem, he encouraged me to become a warrior for my own brain health, to minimize damage and to live a full, long, brain-healthy life. What I have come to realize is that what is good for the body and the heart is also vitally good for our noggin. Dr. Amen has suggested that I take some specialized supplements that target, heal, and help brain function. My diet had to change pretty drastically. Sugar, apparently, does not love our brain any more than it loves our stomach and thighs. He also suggested I do some brain exercises online, but he emphasized over and over again: physical exercise will be one of my greatest weapons in keeping young of mind and youthful in body, at any age. As it turns out, dancing—the only exercise I really enjoy—is one of the best ways to keep the brain sharp. This is because it not only is aerobic but also involves coordination, learning and remembering new steps, and synchronizing movements to the beat of music—all activities that encourage new neurons to grow, even as our muscles grow and stretch.

In my case, we also discovered that my brain had suffered some injury because of early exposure to mold, lead, and mercury. This means I have to be especially proactive about my brain health if I want to avoid things like early onset dementia or Alzheimer's. It's, frankly, a little overwhelming. However, I have drastically changed my habits, and therefore my life, before, so I know I can do it again. Back when I was in seminary, I began to struggle with a dark cloud of chemical depression. I set a small goal: to be out of bed by noon and walking outside by 2:00 p.m. (And if you think that sounds ridiculously easy, you've never suffered from a chemical depression.) I began with these small, doable baby steps, and gradually, the more I moved and the faster the pace, the better I began to feel. Now we know that exercise is one of the world's best antidepressants, with nothing but positive side-effects.

In fact, there's not a lot that goes wrong in our lives that a little movement and fresh air can't help. If exercise were a pill, we would be shouting its benefits from the mountaintops. If you and your beloved want to live long, happy, vibrant, passionate lives, there are few better gifts you can give yourself and each other than the gift of staying active.

On Dr. Amen's blog, he shares several benefits of exercise that might perk your interest as you think about the passion that being more fit can bring to your life.

> Exercise improves the flow of oxygen, blood, and nutrients to the brain. It reduces stress, improves your mood, and lowers blood pressure and blood sugar levels, while decreasing inflammation, fat cells, weight, and frailty. At the same time, it increases metabolism, longevity, bone density, and an overall sense of well-being.
>
> *Walking.* Work up to "walking like you're late" 45 minutes a day, 4 times a week. Dr. Amen likes to add "bursting" to his walks. During the walk, take four or five one-minute periods to "burst" (walking or running as fast as you can), then go back to walking. Short-burst training helps raise endorphins, lift your mood, and make you feel more energized.

Strengthen. Did you know that the stronger you are as you age, the less likely you are to get Alzheimer's disease? It's true! A study from Canada found that resistance training plays a role in preventing cognitive decline. On top of that, it also helps with losing weight and belly fat. Dr. Amen typically recommends doing two 35- to 45-minute strength (or resistance) training sessions a week—one for the lower body (abs, lower back, and legs), the other for the upper body (arms, upper back, and chest).

Coordination Activities. Dancing, tennis and other racket sports, and table tennis (the world's best brain sport) are really fun, and they boost activity in the cerebellum—located in the back bottom part of the brain. While the cerebellum is only 10 percent of the brain's volume, it contains 50 percent of our brain cells. It's involved with both physical and thought coordination. [The other benefit of these sports is they require a partner, and if your mate is willing to join you for a round of ping-pong, a game of tennis, or doing the cha-cha-cha, all the better.]

Mindfulness Exercise. Activities such as yoga and tai chi have been found to reduce anxiety and depression AND increase focus. Believe it or not, these calming activities actually burn calories while increasing strength and flexibility and helping you feel centered and grounded.[11]

THE "PHYSICALLY ACTIVE/PASSIONATELY ACTIVE" CONNECTION

Have you ever noticed that after a hard workout or a hike or swim together, you feel more physically attracted to and sexually interested in each other?

That is because there is a strong correlation between being physically active and feeling romantically, passionately inclined.

Because Greeks are among the most physically active people in the world (particularly on islands, where walking hilly terrain is a part of life), perhaps it is no great surprise that Greece ranks atop the list of the world's most sexually active nations, with its people averaging 164 sessions of lovemaking a year, or more than three times a week.

There's no doubt that exercise increases the sex drive for men and women. One study revealed that men who exercised for an hour, three to five days a week, developed a significantly more reliable, enjoyable, and active sex life.[12]

Exercise has sexual side-benefits for the ladies as well. A 2008 study published in the *Journal of Sexual Medicine* revealed that intense, short-duration exercise (twenty minutes, with a target heart rate of 70 percent) significantly enhances the physiological sexual arousal of women.[13]

Of course, the aesthetic gains in a healthier, more toned, and slimmer body often lead to more confidence in the bedroom as you feel more attractive and in the mood for making love.

BENEFITS OF EXERCISING TOGETHER

According to one article, "A growing group of experts agree that couples who exercise together can not only stave off the extra pounds that are often linked to marriage, but they can strengthen their relationship and their sex life, and possibly live happily ever after."[14]

One of the things that help bring Misty and me together emotionally is to get away, go outside, and play! One winter, we found a place in Breckenridge, Colorado, that specialized in snowmobiling. That might not sound like much exercise, but you'd be surprised! Because snowmobiling is not something we'd done before, there was a real sense of adventure, a bit of risk about the activity. When couples do something new together, it can spark feel-good endorphins that draw them together in interdependence.

Dr. Jane Greer, a marriage and relationship psychotherapist, explained, "When a couple works out together, the actual exercise itself can physically and emotionally have a positive impact. Both partners come away with feelings of synchronicity, cooperative spirit and shared passion."[15] *Synchronicity* and *cooperative spirit* are other words for the attunement we talked about in chapter 2. It's fascinating to note that shared passion can arise from exercising together, in any way, shape, or form.

Add in the endorphin boost that comes with exercise, and your mood may be at a high level, resulting in more positive communication. Sweating it out as a couple can reduce stress and produce good moods in both of you, enhancing the way you feel when you are together.

Finally, couples who exercise together are much more likely to stick to their workout goals. One study showed that after twelve months, only 6.3 percent of married couples who exercised together dropped out of their workout routine, while a whopping 43 percent of singles did.[16]

Though Misty and I have been able to go on varied adventures and love it, the thing we do most often, that costs the least and can be easily enjoyed by everyone, is walking. The two knee surgeries took it out of me for a while, but now I'm back on my feet, and we love walking together again. Because I've been able to stay pretty fit for several decades, people are surprised to learn that this was not always the case for me. In fact, it was a huge area of struggle. When I was in my twenties, I smoked and ate thousands of calories a day, and this didn't exactly spur me on to exercise. As I mentioned earlier, depression was my companion in those days, and it was just easier to stay in bed. Forcing myself to walk every day was the first change I made, which ushered in other healthy habits and eventually lifted my depression. I once met a woman whose real name was Happy Walker, and that is what I became back then. Still today, one of the ways Misty and I stay connected emotionally while getting some exercise is by walking together regularly.

It's important to find something you both enjoy equally and can do together. Walking, hiking, riding bikes, dancing, tennis, and swimming are easy for most couples to do together. Some couples love the competitive spirit of being on a soccer or volleyball team. Others might enjoy a calming yoga or tai chi class. Consider working out, and at least occasionally exercising together, as a gift of health to yourselves and an investment in a more passionate relationship. "The secret of change," wrote Socrates, "is to focus all your energy not on fighting the old, but on building the new." Try to think of becoming more active not as fighting against your inner couch potato but as a new adventure in discovering the more vital and energetic you!

If exercise or sports are just not your thing, consider a hobby you both love that involves physical movement. We have friends who love shopping thrift stores and estate sales, then bringing their finds home and refinishing or repurposing old pieces of furniture to bring them new life. The hobby involves lots of walking, lifting, bending, twisting, and old-fashioned elbow grease, but because they are so caught up in the fun of finding and creating treasures, they hardly realize they are (shhhhh) *exercising*.

Maybe the two of you could decide on a project you'd like to do: painting a room, digging a fishpond, planting a garden, building some bookshelves, cleaning out the garage—anything that syncs being active with the fun of creativity and the feeling of mutual accomplishment. In nice weather, dream about ways you could use the sum of your sweat equity to spruce up the backyard with a fountain, a gazebo, a homemade picnic table, or a pretty retaining wall. Take some time off in the evenings to bike to the park or play Frisbee or walk the dog, if you have one. (If you don't have a dog, consider the benefits of getting one. They are cheaper than a personal trainer and may yield just as many fitness rewards, not to mention the calming, happy endorphins that pets bring to their owners.) Think like a kid and go outside to play—with your kids or grandkids. Adding to the benefits of hostessing and cooking that we gleaned in chapter 3, preparing for a party, serving food and drinks, and cleaning up afterward can be almost aerobic! It all adds up to exercise. If you combine movement with fun or getting stuff done, it may be easier to motivate yourself to get up off the couch.

THINK LIKE A GREEK

When you read about the Ikarians in the opening story to this chapter, what aspects of their lives appealed to you most? The Greek philosopher Aristotle said, "We are what we repeatedly do. Excellence, then, is not an act, but a habit." If you want to grow young and stay passionate all your married lives, then it may be time to take inventory of your habits and see where some could use a little tweaking, taking a cue or two from those healthy Greek island elders. Are you getting enough rest? Does your life allow for a short nap a few times a week? Do you have any days set aside when you can wake naturally, without an alarm? Are you connected to friends and family? (Could you be more proactive, perhaps, in reaching out and making those connections?) Do you have a sense of belonging in a local faith community? Are there any foods or beverages in the Ikarian diet that you might like to incorporate into yours? Do you have routines and rituals that give structure and comfort to your day? Do you have time to contemplate the bigger issues of life and talk about them together as a couple? Do you move and work or exercise physically with a portion of your day? Can you let go of stress when your day is done? Do you prioritize sex and lovemaking?

Most couples can really benefit from a vacation away together, and we encourage every couple to, if at all possible, get creative and plan and budget for some sort of honeymoon getaway every year or two. Don't overplan these romantic vacation times. Make sure you allow days when you can forget to look at the clock, forget what day it is, not have to be anywhere at any specific hour. Our "work" on vacation is typically more physical than cerebral and more like play: fishing, kayaking, hiking, walking, swimming, skiing, or snorkeling. Vacation sex is a much-anticipated benefit of getaways! When couples are relaxed, have detached from their to-do lists, are more rested, and have the luxury of slowing down and enjoying each other, they can savor each other and revel in gourmet sex versus quickies. Vacation slows us down and heightens our senses so that everything, including lovemaking, seems elevated and more memorable.

The Greek philosopher Plato said, "The greatest wealth is to be content with little." And Socrates warned to "beware the barrenness of a busy life." Passion, it seems, needs space to grow. We as couples may need to do less, detach more, simplify our lives where we can so that we have the margin needed to deeply nourish ourselves and our marriages, in all the meanings of that word. So many exhausted and overwhelmed married couples feel a deep call in their heart to return to the basics that feed the well-being of body and soul.

So at least a couple times a year, think like a Greek islander. Stop the pressure, the hurry, the schedule. Leave your watches and iPhones behind. Replace the noise in your head with the sound of the ocean or a breeze through the trees. Use your body to swim, walk, make love, and play, and give your overtaxed brain a rest. Eat when you are hungry, sleep when you are tired, dance when you feel like dancing. And get reacquainted with a feeling called passion for life and for each other.

I remembered those early summer mornings seated by a table by the beach sipping a Greek coffee and breathing in the smell of the tamarisk trees and listening to the soft slap of waves against the side of a caique; the lazy oregano-scented lunches, after which Danielle and I would go back to our house to take a nap within the wonderful coolness of our thick-walled farmhouse and, with the children asleep, perhaps make love; and those evenings with the outside world narrowed down to the few yards illuminated by the taverna's lights.

—TOM STONE, *THE SUMMER OF MY GREEK TAVERNA*

Thirteen Ways to Keep Your Love Healthy into Old Age

1. Decide on a project you want to accomplish together, perhaps something to redo, make, or build around the house, that will require some physical exertion and cooperation. In fact, make a list of projects, if you can, that you'd like to work on throughout the year. Projects that will motivate you both to get moving!

2. Set aside as many days per week as possible to allow yourselves to wake naturally. If you have small children, take turns letting each other sleep in at least one day a week. It's not just a luxury; it's a healthy indulgence.

3. Enjoy guilt-free naps. People who have trained themselves to take even short power naps swear by the energy it gives them. If you can't go to sleep in the afternoon, at least set aside ten to twenty minutes to relax completely. Lie down if possible and let go of the cares of the world. You'll be amazed at how this sacred rest in the middle of the day will energize you and renew your passion for the rest of the day.

4. Try incorporating some of the elements of the Greek diet into your life. If you enjoy feta and goat cheese, you may want to use these more often in your menu plans and reap the benefits of their probiotic activity in your digestive system. If you are feeling adventurous, you can buy Greek coffee online (but you'll also need to look up how to make it, as it is more like mud than brewed coffee). Also, bags of Greek mountain tea herbs are available through Amazon. Or research and try a variety of healthy teas and coffees. If you enjoy wine, take a wine-tasting or wine-making class together.

5. Watch *My Big Fat Greek Wedding* together one night, and enjoy the laughter! Talk about which aspects of Greek families might drive you crazy and which ones you love and wish you might have more of in your life, marriage, and family.

6. Look up Mediterranean vegetarian recipes and try a few to see if you can incorporate more vegetables and beans into your diet. If you like eggplant, try the Greek recipe for moussaka! Stuff pita bread with a variety of veggies, goat cheeses, olives, and a small amount of meat, with a little olive oil and vinegar–based dressing.

7. Taking regular walks together is one of the simplest ways to get exercise and catch up on the news of the day. Walk to a juice bar or coffee shop to reward yourselves with a refreshing drink and healthy snack. If the weather is cold, you may want to create a simple home gym, or go to a local gym together three times a week for workout dates, or walk around a big mall, rewarding yourselves with a healthy smoothie at a kiosk when you're done. Another idea is to pick a race for fun or for a cause. Training together for something, whether it's a 5K run or a marathon, can be especially bonding. Even if you aren't running side by side the whole time, encouraging each other and sharing workouts can be a great way to stay close. Explore a new city, push your bodies for a healthy accomplishment, and make a vacation out of it!

8. Consider getting bicycles—perhaps racing bikes, mountain bikes, or old-fashioned cruising bikes (becoming more popular as boomers age)—that you can ride together to and from activities or places you enjoy. Challenge yourselves to see how often you could forego the car and bike to where you want to go. As an aside, Dutch researchers have found that the method

of transport that most boosts the emotion of joy is cycling. So if you can bike from one spot to the next, you'll not only get healthier but also feel happier. Especially if you bike with your sweetie!

9. If you enjoy the water, try going on vacations to warm-weather getaways where you can swim, snorkel, scuba dive, kayak, sail, surf, sailboard, or fish together. Or simply walk along the beach, hand in hand. Water has a way of both relaxing and invigorating couples, with all the physical activities and beauty to be enjoyed around it. In a Harvard University study of 160 male and female swimmers in their forties and sixties, regular physical activity was associated with more frequency and enjoyment of sex. Swimmers in their sixties reported sex lives comparable to those in their forties.[17]

10. Take dance classes together, or simply go dancing and do your own thing. Both the movement and the music add feelings of passion to your lives. When a song you love starts to play, drop what you are doing and waltz your wife around the kitchen, or do a little salsa step in the living room. Have fun! Attend ethnic festivals in which dance is part of the culture, and join in the celebration.

11. Talk about your sense of purpose and meaning, both as individuals and as a couple. Do you belong to a community of faith that supports why you are here on this planet? Is there something God is calling you to do together? Take time to pray together and ask God to reveal what your mission and focus should be. (Often this is where your talents and passion meet the world's needs.) Life without meaning, or without knowing your purpose on earth, becomes dull and boring, no matter how rich you may be in worldly goods. There is nothing that ups

the passion in life like feeling the smile of God on your work, your art, your human connections.

12. Consider having meals with others instead of eating drive-through meals alone in the car. Go to a place with a great salad bar for lunch with your mate or your friend. Don't dine alone every day; go out with others for breakfast or a noon meal at least a couple times a week. Invite others over for a game of cards along with some easy appetizers and wine, or spontaneously ask neighbors to drop over for coffee and dessert. Become a welcoming couple, expanding your table to include family and friends when you can. Yes, it is a little work to prepare, serve, and clean up when you have folks over, but think of all the natural exercise you are getting, along with mood and health benefits that enrich your lives and your passion for people.

13. Try a new sport or physical activity together, something you've never done before. A small risk and sense of adventure heightens the feeling of being alive. You could hike to a new place, try going on a zip line, learn to play tennis, or take an exercise class (yoga, spin, dance, or water aerobics, for example). Set up a volleyball net, a badminton net, or a croquet course in the backyard during warm months, to encourage the whole family to bend, stretch, and move.

CHAPTER 8

THE SECRET OF BLENDING THE SACRED AND THE SEXUAL

Many waters cannot quench love, nor can rivers drown it. If a man tried to buy love with all his wealth, his offer would be utterly scorned.

—SONG OF SOLOMON 8:7 NLT

<hr />

My favorite Mediterranean country, by far, is Israel. Misty and I have both visited the Holy Land, separately. It is a goal to take each of our kids on an international trip with us as they reach their senior year in high school. I took our oldest, Madeline, to Israel and baptized her in the Jordan River. I took Carter with me to Australia on a speaking engagement. Next in line was James, whom I took with me on an excursion to Israel and Jordan. One morning, James and I enjoyed a cup of coffee in our tent in Petra, Jordan, where we were camped across from the famous stone-carved temple where several iconic scenes from *Indiana Jones and the Last Crusade* were filmed. Later, I had the privilege of baptizing James, as well, in the Jordan River, followed by a fascinating tour of the excavation of King Solomon's Gate at Tel Gezer.

Misty and I have always been fascinated with King Solomon, who penned three of our favorite books of the Bible: Ecclesiastes, Proverbs, and Song of Songs—more often called the Song of Solomon. And in fact this is why we named our son Solomon. King Solomon was known for his great wisdom, and his name means "peace." Ecclesiastes is a book written about Solomon's search for meaning in his all-access life; he finds in his most sane observations that there is no other conclusion but to fear God and keep his commands (Eccl. 12:13). Proverbs is a book filled with practical wisdom for leading a balanced, meaningful life with God. And Song of Solomon is a book that is unashamedly written in praise of deep, committed, faithful love, and sex—rapturous sex, sex the way God intended it, sex that bonds a couple and breaks down barriers as nothing else can, sex that leaves you better, fuller, "healed-er," and coming back for more.

KING SOLOMON'S ODE TO SENSUAL LOVE

King Solomon was said to have written a thousand poems, but the one that made it into the Old Testament is thought to be the *creme de la creme* of his love poems: Song of Songs. In its simplest interpretation, it is a love poem to the first love of Solomon's life, the Shulamite woman who became his wife. You can't help but notice that Solomon spares no ink in writing about the alluring body of his beautiful bride, from tip to toe. And she responds too, praising his masculine form in kind. Of his bride, Solomon writes,

> *Behold, you are beautiful, my love,*
> *behold, you are beautiful!*
> *Your eyes are doves*
> *behind your veil.*
> *Your hair is like a flock of goats*
> *leaping down the slopes of Gilead.*
> *Your teeth are like a flock of shorn ewes*

> *that have come up from the washing,*
> *all of which bear twins,*
> > *and not one among them has lost its young.*
> *Your lips are like a scarlet thread,*
> > *and your mouth is lovely.*
> *Your cheeks are like halves of a pomegranate*
> > *behind your veil.*
> *Your neck is like the tower of David,*
> > *built in rows of stone;*
> *on it hang a thousand shields,*
> > *all of them shields of warriors.*
> *Your two breasts are like two fawns,*
> > *twins of a gazelle,*
> > *that graze among the lilies.*

—SONG OF SOLOMON 4:1–5 ESV

Solomon's bride is equally lavish with metaphors to praise her husband's body.

> *My beloved is white and ruddy,*
> *Chief among ten thousand.*
> *His head is like the finest gold;*
> *His locks are wavy,*
> *And black as a raven.*
> *His eyes are like doves*
> *By the rivers of waters,*
> *Washed with milk,*
> *And fitly set.*
> *His cheeks are like a bed of spices,*
> *Banks of scented herbs.*
> *His lips are lilies,*
> *Dripping liquid myrrh.*
> *His hands are rods of gold*

Set with beryl.
His body is carved ivory
Inlaid with sapphires.
His legs are pillars of marble
Set on bases of fine gold.
His countenance is like Lebanon,
Excellent as the cedars.
His mouth is most sweet,
Yes, he is altogether lovely.
This is my beloved,
And this is my friend.

—SONG OF SOLOMON 5:10–16 NKJV

In this poem are dozens of beautiful metaphors for all the sensual and sexual parts of the human body.

And God says this is good! God created us and wired us for pleasure!

I can't help but wonder what trouble Solomon might have avoided, and what beautiful love poems he might have continued to write, had he plumbed the depths and loveliness of this one woman for a lifetime. But even the wisest man on earth let his riches and his power go unchecked until he had accumulated no less than seven hundred wives and three hundred concubines. And the Scriptures say that later on, "sure enough, they turned his heart away from the Lord, especially in his old age. They encouraged him to worship their gods instead of trusting completely in the Lord as his father David had done" (1 Kings 11:3–4 TLB). Most of Solomon's wisdom came to him late in life, when he would pen the book of Proverbs. And in this book, a letter to his son, he almost begs his own boy to be wiser in love than he was. Solomon urges his son to "be happy, yes, rejoice in the wife of your youth. Let her breasts and tender embrace satisfy you. Let her love alone fill you with delight" (Prov. 5:18–19 TLB). Note that Solomon does not say "wives"; he says "wife." Sometimes wisdom comes in hindsight, from years of wrong turns and detours and experiencing the consequences that follow. I believe that

Solomon regretted adding so many wives to his harem in his insatiable search for pleasure—and forever looked back with poignancy and fondness to the days of his youth and the pure, free, fabulous, innocent, God-blessed, sacred love and sex between one young king who was head over heels in love and his Shulamite bride. If Solomon had put as much energy into his relationship with his first wife as he did into building his kingdom, his harem, and his ego, he might have found the happiness that eluded him for so many years. His book Ecclesiastes is about the futility of "chasing after the wind" of accumulated wealth and sexual excess; it's a warning that a life without God at the center is meaningless.

PASSION FEEDS PASSION

We've talked a lot about how passion in all of life increases our desire for each other. But the opposite is also true: sex between a loving husband and wife sends passionate ripple effects into the rest of our life. God set up a looping system that continuously fills us with passionate, happy, energizing, and calming hormones to keep us connected to each other and loving our lives. And when life kicks you in the teeth, you may want to read further before going straight for an antidepressant. Because loving sex can be exactly what the doctor ordered to ease emotional pain and feel joy again. One of the reasons why both the Bible (Old and New Testament) and the Talmud (orthodox rabbinical teachings and laws) encourage couples to come together in regular lovemaking is that sex is a gift from God to us that keeps on giving in an endless cycle of upward-spiraling well-being. Loving sex increases both our energy and our desire to live with passion, and when we are fully enjoying and savoring life, we find ourselves desiring sex more.

HEALTH PERKS OF SEXUAL PASSION

Touching, kissing, and making love all release hormones into our system that flood us with positive energy and increase our passion for the day. Ever notice how after sex in the morning, a man is suddenly ready to go "kill the bear," or tackle a project at work? It can sometimes hurt a woman's feelings, how quickly a guy can go from lovemaking to having a burst of enthusiasm about getting started on a project. It's not that a husband gets what he wants and then gets bored with his wife and is ready to change gears. It's that his wife has filled his physical, emotional, and mental tank and put a spring in his step that makes him feel like he can conquer the world. At night, however, sexual release often allows a man to fall into a deep, satisfied sleep. A wife's body in loving motion has so much power to energize her husband and increase his confidence—and to be a comforting, soft place to land when he needs to unwind.

In addition to the emotional perks, there are health and longevity benefits as well. For example, sex three times a week has been found to cut a man's risk of heart attack in half; it has been shown to help prevent prostate cancer; and men who have frequent orgasms live significantly longer than men who have sex infrequently. (Remember those long-living, sexually active Ikarians?) No doubt about it—regular sex is good medicine for a man.

But it may surprise you to learn that sex is equally good, if not even better, medicine for a woman.

Women, after sex, often feel more calm and connected to their man as the "cuddling hormone" of oxytocin is released. In fact, studies show that after intercourse, many women feel a euphoric lift in their mood and find they have less physical and emotional pain. Indeed, the oxytocin released by a woman's orgasm relaxes her, acts as a mild pain reliever, and helps even out menstrual issues. The orgasmic rush of blood through her body helps eliminate many toxins. And if that isn't motivating enough, a study conducted at the Royal Edinburgh Hospital found that women who had frequent orgasms looked, on average, ten years younger.[1]

Jewish Rules for Sex That May Surprise You

Here are some interesting rabbinical teachings about sex in marriage. What I found fascinating is how woman-centered sex is supposed to be in the Jewish culture, how it is all about her pleasure. Perhaps because if a woman is delighted with and enjoying lovemaking, the man will automatically be ecstatic.

A man never forces his wife to have sex.

A husband and wife may never have sex while drunk or quarreling.

It's a serious offense to use sex to punish or manipulate a spouse.

Sex is a woman's right, and not a man's right.

A man has a duty to give sex to his wife regularly and ensure that sex is pleasurable for her.

Sex may never be used as a weapon, either to deprive your mate of it or to compel them to have it. No pushy persuasions, no threats. Using sex as a manipulation is seen as simply wrong and sinful.

The man is obligated to watch for signs of his wife wanting touching, intimacy, and consummation—and to offer her pleasure without her having to ask.

Sex is one of the woman's three basic rights in marriage which a husband may not reduce.

And the Talmud specifies the quality and quantity of sex that a man must give his wife.

A husband may not vow to abstain from sex for an extended period of time.

A husband's consistent refusal to engage in sexual relations is grounds for divorce.

> He may not take a journey for an extended period of
> time, because that would deprive the wife of a sexual
> relationship. In fact, one ancient text says that if a man has
> an opportunity to earn more money, but it would mean
> traveling away from his wife rather than working around
> the village, she has the right to tell him no. If she doesn't
> want him to go because it would destroy or weaken the
> marital bond, he cannot go.[2]
>
> In many pockets of Judaism, the women are raised to value their
> libidos and to see themselves as highly sensual creatures who will
> need and want to be pleasured regularly by their husband. They are
> taught that it is a joyful, holy, and sacred act, honoring to God. The
> general view of the culture is that a woman's hunger is greater than
> a man's. What an interesting twist and departure from the Western
> mindset!

And you thought age-defying miracles came in expensive bottles of beauty lotion.

Turns out that the best de-aging beautifier comes free of charge, in the comfort of your own husband's arms.

A final interesting nuance to note is the way a woman can find fulfillment in providing sensual love and connection for her husband to rest in. Misty and I share a private reference, which will now on this page become not so private. But when I am feeling out of sorts and restless, Misty will notice, and with pity in her voice and inviting eyes, she will suggest, "Perhaps it's time for some therapy." I love her for knowing that when I may be feeling disconnected and a bit lost, entering into a time of lovemaking and connecting to my wife will reorient me, helping me to feel loved, received, and accepted at the deepest level. These sweet times provide a settling to my soul, with the one I love most.

LOVEMAKING: A JEWISH PERSPECTIVE

There's a phrase in the Old Testament that many see as a euphemism for sex. It's the phrase "they knew each other." But what this means to the Hebrew mind is that each time a couple makes love, they come to know each other a little more deeply. Their bodies and their souls meet and melt together. The physical and the emotional coincide, and the couple experiences deeper and deeper oneness, or—as we spoke about in chapter 2—deeper attunement.

Have you ever had a soulish experience during sex? A moment when you looked into each other's eyes and felt that you were joining not only two bodies but also two hearts? This is gourmet sex: a blending of the sacred and the sexual. Remember back in chapter 4 when I theorized that America is addicted to junk food not because we value food too much but because we value it too little? When food is honored and savored, we don't settle for a drive-through cheeseburger and fries. Foodies tend to celebrate and delight in all the moments that lead up to the meal—the farmer's market, the prep, the cooking, the serving, and finally the moment when they get to taste all they've worked for and anticipated. In a similar way, I believe thousands are addicted to internet porn not because they value sex and enjoy it too much but because they value and enjoy it too little. They are having drive-through sex instead of intimate, gourmet, God-blessed sex. Lovemaking with your best friend, your soulmate and playmate, is more than physical fun; it is wholly, holy pleasure. It permeates every cell in your body, making you feel glad to be alive!

SEX AS MITZVAH

In the Christian tradition, we have holy sacraments in our churches—things like Communion and baptism. In the Jewish tradition, such holy acts or rituals are called "mitzvahs"—ceremonies that remind people of, and bond them more deeply to, God. In Judaism, lovemaking is considered a mitzvah, a holy ritual between husband and wife, given by God to regularly bind them closer to one another and to him. Christians take Holy Communion to remember Christ's sacrifice and love for us. And in remembering how loved and forgiven we are, we come away from the table of bread and wine refreshed in spirit. In the Hebrew tradition, men and women experience a mitzvah—a holy communion of body, mind, and soul—in lovemaking. And they come away from the marriage bed renewed and refreshed on every level.

One of the sacred rituals of Judaism involves the keeping of the Sabbath, which begins eighteen minutes before sundown on Friday night. If you've seen the Broadway musical or movie *Fiddler on the Roof*, you may recall the hushed, beautiful, sacred scene in which all work suddenly ceases in the kitchen, all chatter comes to a halt, just before the sun sets. The food has been prepared, the table has been set, and the family gathers around it. The father, Tevye, is wearing his kippah, or prayer cap; the mother, Golda, pulls a lace prayer shawl over her head and lights two candles (one symbolizes "remember the Sabbath," the other "keep it holy"). She slowly waves her hands over the candles three times, a symbol of welcoming Shabbat (the Sabbath) as one would welcome a queen into the home. In the movie, the father and mother sing "A Sabbath Prayer" over their daughters, as a blessing. (Google "Sabbath prayer, Fiddler on the Roof," and a YouTube video of the scene should pop up. If you've not seen it, it really is a beautifully filmed moment, and worth a view to help you imagine the mood around the Shabbat table.)

In traditional Jewish homes, Shabbat opens with a prayer of blessing: "Blessed are you, Lord our God, King of the universe, who has sanctified us with his commandments, and commanded us to kindle the light of the Holy Shabbat." Eyes remain closed as blessings are prayed over the children and for any other needs. Then the husband stands behind his wife, places his hands on her shoulders, and sings over her "Eshet Chayil" ("A Woman of Valor"). This from the last chapter of Proverbs, twenty-two verses that extol the blessing of a good wife, beginning with, "Who can find a virtuous wife? For her worth is far above rubies" (NKJV).

In this way, the husband honors his wife every week, reminding himself and his children of the blessing she is to their lives. I can only imagine how this tradition must elevate a woman's self-esteem, ushering in feelings of warmth and of pride and of connection to her husband, and how it would remind the husband throughout the week of the blessing his wife is to him. (This must also make a man think about how he treats his wife Sunday through Thursday.)

Later, in the privacy of their room, a traditional Jewish couple will read portions of the Song of Solomon to each other and then make love. In fact, ancient rabbis would give a benediction encouraging all married couples to make love on Shabbat as preparation for worship Sabbath morning. Do you see this beautiful mixing of the sacred and the sexual? How one spurs on the other? The Shabbat ceremony prepares a couple to slow down, to put aside work and busyness, to enjoy a good meal—to create the conditions prime for lovemaking. Then, unhurried lovemaking on Friday evening prepares the couple to more fully enjoy the Sabbath (Saturday) of rest and worship, of feeling emotionally, spiritually, and physically connected to each other throughout the day.

Can you imagine the petty disagreements couples might avoid if they knew that every Friday evening the world would come to a standstill? And that Saturday would be unhurried as well, the gift of a whole day to worship, read, talk, nap, munch on leftovers (no cooking)—with no pressure to catch up on laundry or pay bills or even mow the lawn. I'm guessing this ritual alone would put many marriage therapists out of business. Marriage therapist and brain expert Dr. Earl Henslin wrote about this delightful memory, shared by one of his female clients, in the book *This Is Your Brain in Love*.

> When I was in elementary school my favorite girlfriend was Jewish. I just loved it when I stayed over at her house on Friday nights. Every Friday night we would have dinner in the dining room, and the best china was out. The dad would come home from work, then he'd go upstairs and shower and completely change into a nice outfit. Then the

mom would go upstairs, shower and come down in a beautiful dress, and I remember she wore a lacey veil over her face.

The moment the mom stepped into the dining room, the dad got up, pulled out a chair, and she sat down. I just loved watching him being so gallant to his wife. And then came prayers, and Scriptures. When we finished dinner, we watched the parents go upstairs, arm in arm, gazing at each other like lovesick teenagers. The kids would then start giggling as they took the plates into the kitchen and started washing dishes as they'd been taught to do on Fridays, to allow their parents their "alone time."[3]

This scene alone could be enough to tempt many Christian wives to convert to Judaism! But better yet, why not adopt some of the elements of the Jewish tradition, which is also our Christian heritage, and bring it into our homes?

As you know, I am all for saving up and searching for specials and bargains online so you can enjoy romantic getaways. But how we treat each other as a couple at home, day in and day out, is even more important. Not only for our own sakes but also for our children, who are watching us demonstrate what a good marriage looks like every day. If the kids wake up every morning and see me and their mother in our living room, reading the Bible, sharing with each other, and showing our love for God and one another, they come to rely on the solidarity of our connection. You know the old saying that more is caught than taught? Children will not hear the words you tell them, if you are not living them out before their eyes. When I see that Misty is up against a deadline or feeling overloaded, the kids will see their dad take over the kitchen, prepare dinner, and make their school lunches with a cheerful attitude. They also see us flirt and dance and have fun. They see us casually touch or kiss, or wink and give knowing smiles to each other. Nothing Misty or I could say will prepare them for a good marriage as much as what we do and how we behave in front of them.

THE MYSTERY OF MODESTY

*The whole problem with marriage is, it's so darn legal.
It's available to us. So in Jewish law, the forbidden is
mixed into the legal, and it makes for a much more
erotic marriage.*

—RABBI SHMUEL BOTEACH

Imagine what sex with your wife might have been like in biblical times. Men were not constantly stimulated by (or numb to) the ubiquitous sight of a woman's scantily clad body assaulting him from billboards, TV, and just a stroll through the mall. Men didn't see much of a woman's form at all under long robes and veils and, of course, the strict cultural codes of modesty.

Then the husband comes home and sees his wife casually lift her shawl to reveal a shoulder. Slips out of her shift to reveal more of the glory of her female form. And what she is doing is unwrapping the *only* body of the only naked woman he will have the pleasure of viewing, ever. His wife's soft skin will be the only woman's skin he will touch; he has no other comparisons in mind that compete with his wife. She is his alone and worthy of honor, and if he cherishes her, as we hope any man would, she feels treasured. She loves that he looks and admires her, she does not feel objectified, because he is simply adoring a treasure and not comparing her with others, degrading or using her.

You may have heard of Rabbi Shmuel "Shmuley" Boteach, one of the most popular, influential (and controversial) rabbis in America today. He had a radio and TV show (*Shalom in the Home*) and has authored thirty-three books, including several on the subject of marriage and passion from a Jewish perspective. And he is anything but shy about talking about why he believes that many of the Jewish traditions and holy practices are actually secrets to a more passionate life as husband and wife. In addition to the general codes of modesty in orthodox Jewish marriages, there are twelve days out of every month when a Jewish wife is unavailable for sex with her husband. And this often includes no kissing or hand-holding. Nothing physical. However, they can talk intimately about anything.

There are several perks to this, Rabbi Shmuley asserts. During the twelve days when a man's wife is as unavailable to him as a stranger would be, there is a hunger for the forbidden that makes everything more erotic. He writes, "Suddenly, you're working to catch glimpses of your wife when she is in the shower. You're studying the black lacy bra she left outside the shower. . . . Before, when she is permitted to you, she would walk around the room naked and you would read the *Wall Street Journal*. Now, when she bends over fully clothed, you're sneaking glimpses of her cleavage. Cool. And hot. Imagine that."[4]

Trust me, I'm not willing to forfeit intimacy with my wife for two weeks out of each month, but I do believe that couples can maintain a certain air of mystery, at least now and then, to keep passion percolating in their marriage. When a couple has to overcome challenges in order to be with one another, it heightens the fun (and relief!) of finally getting to be together. (Children create these challenges for many couples on a remarkably regular basis.) Couples who excel at the art of flirting are maintaining a playful element of the chase in their marriage, and they may unconsciously use elements of the forbidden to increase desire.

What does playful mysteriousness and hints of the forbidden look like in a committed marriage? Here are a few ideas to get your creative minds going!

- Wives, tell your husband you'd like to meet him for dinner at a new restaurant you've never tried before. Dress to impress him. Driving there in separate cars can increase the feeling of meeting someone new; it adds the excitement of discovering your mate there at the restaurant, rather than watching each other dress and driving to dinner together. It just adds a small element of discovery and surprise that can increase feelings of passion. Then sometime during dinner, mention that you've packed a bag and booked a local hotel room for the night (and, if you have kids, that you've arranged for them to stay with a friend or relative overnight). There's something about time together in a hotel that is very, very steamy. The unfamiliar room and bed and locale all add to the surprise elements that put us in the mood for love.

- Or the husband might arrange the surprise hotel night and then say to his wife, who may be exhausted from caring for the kids, "I've booked a hotel room for tonight, just for us. And tomorrow morning, I'll go home and take the kids to breakfast and let you enjoy sleeping in. Order breakfast in bed. Take time to rest and pamper yourself." Don't forget to pack her a bag of overnight essentials, or plan to swing by the house to let her throw together a travel bag.

- Meet your husband at his office, late in the day, just before everyone goes home. Bring a little happy hour picnic with you to surprise him. Wear some sexy lingerie under an easy-to-take-off dress. Put a blanket on the floor as if you were about to set out treats for a picnic. Once you are sure the building is clear, lock his office door, slowly slip out of the dress, and let him know that, actually, you will be the first course this evening.

- Add to the overall mystique of you by reading or learning something new and interesting to share. Listen to audiotapes or podcasts or TED talks, go to a conference or seminar to learn about something that fascinates you. In other words, *be* interested in life and learning new things, and you'll remain interesting to others. Your mate will always be wondering what you are thinking about, what you are discovering, and you'll never run out of new things to talk about, new depths to explore.

- Although spending a lot of time together is a blessing in marriage, we also need our times apart to remain a little mysterious. When a wife comes home from a night out with the girls, sounding happy and looking gorgeous, most husbands can't help but wonder, "What did those ladies talk about? Did any men try to flirt with my wife in my absence?" The whole evening is a mystery to him, and this makes his wife suddenly very alluring. When a husband goes off to a men's church retreat, the wife will be dying of curiosity to know what men do and talk about when there are no women around. How do men bond? What do they do for fun? And all this curiosity sparks passionate feelings as well. So time apart, especially if it's time for personal fun, renewal, learning, or growth, allows you more surprising mysteries to discuss when you are together again.

AUTHENTICITY IS ATTRACTIVE

Rabbi Shmuley also believes that the most erotic and charming thing about two people is the openness of their hearts. He believes this is part of what bonded Adam and Eve, in their physically and emotionally innocent state of nakedness in the garden of Eden. The rabbi says about innocent, openhearted people, "Because their souls are translucent you can see right through to their essence. Innocent people disarm us. Because they are so natural they invite us to behave natural around them as well, allowing for our deepest selves to be manifest. Innocence is about living honestly, not pretending to be happy or grieved when we are not." What Shmuley calls "innocence," I might call "authenticity." Either way, what we are talking about is being open, honest, and vulnerable with each other. Normal, healthy children are like this naturally. There's no pretense, no games, no emotional hiding. They are authentic.

Remember how, on our first date, Misty ordered a steak without a shred of self-consciousness? She was who she was. She ordered what she wanted. She never thought about doing it any other way. I think it was her pure, honest, Midwestern way of being that made me fall in love with her. There was no grandstanding, no game playing. She was stunningly beautiful, no doubt. But in Southern California, where values are so often external and women are more concerned about how they appear than about who they really are, Misty blew into my heart like a cool, fresh breeze. I found her mesmerizing.

It is important to be who you really are from the start of romance, so that the person who falls in love with you is falling for the real, authentic you. Have you ever noticed that when the two of you have a real, honest, clear-the-air, soul-baring discussion, you feel more attracted to each other? We are drawn to people who are open and vulnerable and real with us. (A note here: This is why many physical affairs begin with authentic, intimate conversations between friends of the opposite sex. Use this powerful information to create the conditions for ever-increasing intimacy, passion, and romance in your own marriage.) Letting down your guard with each other in loving, honest, vulnerable conversation often leads to both emotional and physical intimacy. A wonderful, natural progression between married friends and lovers.

POLARITY

Rabbi Shmuley believes that in order for attraction to remain strong in a marriage, there has to be a strong polarity, two highly charged and very different magnetic pulls. Men have to feel like men. And women should be glad they are women. Too much homogenization of the sexes in a marriage leads to less sexual tension and attraction between spouses. This is one of the reasons why orthodox Jewish men and women sit separately in synagogue and their children go to all boys' or all girls' schools. This segregation is not done to remove temptation or make one gender more powerful than the other. It is to help keep an air of mystery, specialness, and intrigue about the opposite sex. It is a way to elevate the mystique of both the masculine and the feminine in the culture. Magnets can lose their polarity, their powerful pulls, if they are stored together too often. So the separateness in Jewish culture is actually a way to keep the magnetism between men and women strong.

When God created man and woman, Jews believe, he did so because husband and wife yearned for and needed what each other brought, to create "a more perfect union," so to speak. And this drive for completion is what generates ongoing attraction.

Have you ever observed a relationship in which the pull of attraction had died and there was no more flirting, no more spark? A marriage of friends, perhaps, but you knew they weren't red-hot lovers anymore.

One of my good buddies told me, "In my first marriage, my wife wore sweats to bed every night. I was proud that she was athletic, but she would use her early morning workout as a way to avoid intimacy in the morning. And because she had to rise at 4:00 a.m. to work out, she had to go to bed extra early (7:30 p.m.) so she could rule out lovemaking at night. She had a strong need to be right about everything, and when I'd bring up a subject that was uncomfortable for her, she'd say, 'Give me a break'—and with those words, the subject would be off the table. I learned early in our marriage that it would be futile to push for an open and honest discussion about intimacy. Sex would be on her timetable, once a week on the weekend, or it would not happen at all. If I dared try to flirt, hug, or kiss her on any other day except 'the appointed day for sex,' she would quickly squelch it with a putdown. She criticized me in ways that tore at my manhood. She insisted we pray together—on our knees—every day, which I did, hoping perhaps that spiritual intimacy might one day spill over to physical intimacy. It did nothing to make me feel closer to her as a lover. We enjoyed watching sports together, which could have been a lot of fun if she also enjoyed snuggling together on the couch as we cheered on our favorite teams, or walked hand in hand with me when we went to a ball game. But there was none of that. She never wanted to get 'dolled up,' as lots of women do. I was living in a bland, homogenized marriage, where I felt emasculated and helpless to change the dynamics between us. She didn't know how to make me feel like a man, and I gave up on trying to make her feel like a woman, when all my efforts to do so failed or backfired. Eventually our marriage died, not of anger or drama but of boredom and blandness."

My friend's marriage lost its magnetic charge, if in fact it had ever had one.

I am not saying that femininity always looks like a woman in a dress and heels, admiring her man while batting her eyelashes. Because sometimes femininity looks like a woman on a soccer field scoring a goal. And sometimes masculinity looks like a man changing a baby's diaper or whipping up pancakes. What is important is this: a man must feel like a man, be comfortable in his masculine skin, and a woman needs to help him be glad he is a man. Also, a woman must "enjoy being a girl," love the feminine skin she is in. And her man needs to encourage and honor her feminine gifts. What exactly this might look like from couple to couple may be different, but it is vital that you discover how to keep the magnetic pull strong between you.

Thirteen Ways to Mix the Spiritual and the Sexual with Your Lover

1. Read and study the Song of Solomon together. You may want to read David Hubbard's *Song of Solomon*, Tom Gledhill's *Message of the Song of Songs*, or Jodie Dillow's *Solomon on Sex* to supplement your study. If it feels comfortable, write a love poem to each other, describing what you find most irresistible about one another. I don't know why so many secular workshops so often use the ancient Hindu-based Kama Sutra as their teaching text, and yet seem to ignore one of the most beautiful and best ancient "sex manuals" of all time—the Song of Solomon from the Bible.

2. Create a budget for lingerie. *Garments, robes, finery, clothing, scarves, adornment*—all words we find in Scripture, often surrounding the marriage bed or the beauty of the temple. Wearing something alluring, that hides a woman's body just

enough to enhance her mystery, has been sexy since time began. When a woman is wearing pretty lingerie, she automatically feels sexier. And it goes without saying that men appreciate the effort! Agree together that your sex life is worth the investment. Rather than go on one big shopping spree, consider budgeting for a new piece or two of sexy lingerie every month. This doesn't have to be a budget buster. Shop sales and keep your eyes open for a little somethin' new to make you feel sexy and make his eyes pop.

3. Take turns creating a mystery date for each other. Perhaps the wife can do this one month, the husband the next. If it goes well, continue the tradition.

4. Consider creating your own version of Shabbat, something that works naturally for you both. Perhaps it's an agreement to have dinner and prayer by candlelight on Friday nights, no technology allowed. Or make Friday nights your sacred date night, interrupted only by emergencies. Make sure this date includes time for talking and time for intimacy. There's something very healing and stabilizing about having a custom like Shabbat, a designated time every week to slow the pace and connect with God and with each other.

5. Discuss the whole idea of "Sabbath," and the rest it was created to give us. Are there some ways you can bring the concept of Sabbath rest into your lives? And if so, what would this look like, and how can you incorporate it?

6. Set aside one of your date nights to discuss magnetic sexual polarity. Wives, ask your husband, "What do you love most about being a man? Can you tell me about a time in your life when you felt most emotionally healthy and masculine?"

Husbands, ask your wife, "What do you love most about being a woman? When do you feel most content, happy, and feminine?" Ask each other how you can encourage one another in the area of healthy sexual identity.

7. Consider your own personality and ask yourself, "Am I interesting? Am I fascinated by life?" Are you a man of mystery? A woman of mystique? If you've allowed yourself to become boring, if you are not personally growing or changing or being enthralled by life, do something to fix that. Take a class, learn a skill, dive into a subject you've wanted to explore. Most important, be growing spiritually—through reading and prayer, participating in a Bible study, singing in a choir, reading spiritual books and biographies, or volunteering to help the poor or the sick. Expand your life, spiritually speaking, so that when you come together to make love, you are bringing two spiritually mature and sensitive people to the marriage bed.

8. Together, give thanks for the gift of sex. Now and again in private, just-the-two-of-you moments, thank God for the blessing of this gift of intimacy, the joy of closeness and physical connection.

9. Plan a romantic/spiritual trip to the Holy Land. Discuss how you can combine a sacred, spiritual experience with romance and physical passion.

10. Say a blessing over one another every day. This could be something you say aloud to each other in the morning before you kiss goodbye, something you pray over your mate in their absence, or something you say at dinnertime. (If you have children, include a short blessing for them as well.) There are many beautiful Hebrew blessings; you may find one in a book or online to use for this.

11. If you have sexual baggage or trauma or hurts of any kind, seek out professional, compassionate Christian therapists who can help. Commit to becoming a part of each other's sexual healing, as you embrace God-blessed sex and allow God to heal old wounds.

12. Make liberal use of candles. There is something both sacred and romantic about dining, praying, bathing, or making love by candlelight.

13. Make use of aromas that heighten passion. The use of aromatherapy and essential oil is as old as the Bible (or older). Try aromas that are known to increase desire; use some erotic essential oil mixed with coconut oil to give each other a sensual massage by candlelight. Or use a diffuser to fill the room with a romantic scent. (Scents can be very individual, so test them on one another before filling your bedroom with them. And go lightly with them. Aromas should be very light, not heavy perfumes.) Play soft music in the background. Create a love nest to rival Solomon's! In wedding vows of old, there was the phrase "With my body, I thee worship." How can you, with your body, adore and love and bring pleasure to your mate?

PERSONAL PARTING THOUGHTS

I have been loving you a little more every minute since this morning.

—VICTOR HUGO, *LES MISERABLES*

According to couples therapist John Jacobs, "The single greatest weapon in the battle to ensure the survival of a long-term relationship is maintaining awareness of the fragility of the marital bond."

In other words, people who remain happily, passionately coupled for a lifetime realize how easily a marriage—any marriage, even a marriage of two fine, caring, well-meaning individuals—can go off the rails. And frankly, it can happen in a very short time, if a marriage is not regularly nourished and tended to by both husband and wife. One person can make changes that begin to improve a marriage, but eventually, for long-lasting, passionate love, it takes two to tango.

I have come to believe that the wisest, most passionate couples prioritize their relationship above almost everything else. Right after their personal faith, they choose to have a marriage-centered marriage.

Not a career- or work-centered marriage.

Not a kid-centered marriage.

Not a ministry-centered marriage or a hobby- or sport-centered marriage.

Not a me-centered marriage or a you-centered marriage.

But an us-centered marriage: a marriage-centered marriage.

It is my observation that when couples choose to make their marriage top priority, the rest of life's important issues tend to balance out on their own.

THE WELL-TENDED MARRIAGE

The happiest couples feed their relationship, regularly, with all the ingredients of passion that we've talked about thus far; they lovingly, purposefully tend to their marriage every day in some big or small way.

"Love doesn't just sit there, like a stone," wrote novelist Ursula K. Le Guin. "It has to be made, like bread; remade all the time, made new." In Texas, where I grew up, it was common for mamas and "meemaws" to make the most amazing sourdough bread you've ever tasted, like clockwork every week. Sourdough bread is deliciously yeasty and just slightly sweet, but with a twinge of sour that gives it a special balance of flavor. Served right out of the oven with a smear of real butter, it's a slice of heaven. (And you may also recall that sourdough bread naturally lowers glycemic levels; it was touted as one of the factors that may be keeping those Greek Ikarians healthy and happy. So it not only tastes like heaven but also may help you live longer!)

This wonderful bread began with a "starter," which was a little bubbling concoction of yeast, flour, sugar, and water that sat like a mini-monster in a mason jar in the back of the fridge. To keep the starter going, it had to be fed. Yes, fed like a plant. Or maybe more like a puppy, because you had to feed it every day. The little yeasty beasties were alive, and they survived on daily additions of fresh flour and water, so a good baker would never neglect to feed the starter. If you missed a day, the starter might die and the bread wouldn't rise, and this was a near tragedy. If this happened, you had to start all over again, with a starter you had to beg, borrow, or buy. That was a huge hassle, and you wanted to avoid it.

Marriage is almost as fragile and needy as a sourdough starter. If words of encouragement and praise and love go unsaid for long, a marriage may languish and eventually die from neglect. The damage that can be done in one day by a rejecting or critical spouse can be huge, reducing the feeling of safety and connection for a long time. One wife shared, "My husband told me I was pretty and that he loved me exactly one time, in what would be the last three years of our marriage. I tried to live on the memory of that one compliment, as long as I could, but eventually my heart broke, love died, and so did our marriage." I have heard grown men say things like, "I told her I loved her when I married my wife. I haven't changed my mind, so I don't know why she needs to keep hearing the words over and over again." Of course, most of these grown men are now sleeping single in a double bed.

Suffice it to say that a marriage is a living, breathing thing. Feed it, nourish it, and it will gladden your heart and bless your life with ever-increasing passion and joy. Neglect or abuse it, and love will shrivel and die.

QUICK REVIEW OF THE SEVEN SECRETS

Before we end this book, let's pause for a little recap and take one last look at the list of seven secrets to a more passionate marriage, as we've observed in Mediterranean countries.

1. *The Secret of Attunement.* Connecting to and focusing on each other at some point every day, from the heart.
2. *The Secret of Playfulness.* Enjoying each other through laughter and simply having fun.
3. *The Secret of Savoring Food.* Taking advantage of opportunities to cook, serve, and savor delicious food, as we slow down to share the events of our lives or share deeper thoughts together.

4. *The Secret of Enjoying Beauty.* Purposefully surrounding ourselves with lovely sights, sounds, and smells. Going to inspiring places can feed our soul's hunger for beauty. When we enjoy beauty—in nature, in culture, or in each other—we connect, heart to heart.

5. *The Secret of Creativity.* Giving yourselves the passion-boosting pleasure of working on projects together or engaging in an activity that brings you both into a sense of flow. So much passion arises from that special feeling of being in the zone, working in tandem on something that uses your creativity and talents.

6. *The Secret of Health and Longevity.* Prioritizing rest, natural exercise, healthy food, sexual intimacy, a sense of belonging to community, and growing in a vibrant faith.

7. *The Secret of Blending the Sacred and Sexual.* Enjoying mind-blowing, God-blessed sex that is both physically pleasurable and spiritually bonding.

I would urge you to print out two copies of the above list (you can find a printable copy of it on my website at Newlife.com) and put it someplace where you can see it often. Perhaps tape it to your bathroom mirror or to the dash of your car, or tuck it into your Bible. As you familiarize yourself with these seven secrets to passion, you'll naturally start looking for ways to apply them to your life and marriage.

I would also suggest that after reading this book, you and your mate sit down together and look over the seven secrets and talk about which areas you'd most like to work on. Begin with the area you both agree deserves the most attention—or maybe the one that sounds like the most fun! Give at least one or two weeks to focusing on this secret and applying some of the suggestions from its chapter into your daily lives. Get that plate spinning, so to speak. Then move on to the other six secrets, one at a time, applying what you've learned.

You will be amazed at how quickly these positive experiences will bring relief and healing and feelings of joy and passion back to your marriage.

For other resources and ideas on how to implement the contents of this book or lead a group exploring these life-altering secrets, go to Newlife.com, click on "Mediterranean Love Plan," and download guides for one-on-one and group discussions. And let me hear from you, please, at SArterburn@newlife.com.

PASSION IS PROACTIVE!

Leonardo da Vinci said, "It had long since come to my attention that people of accomplishment rarely sat back and let things happen to them. They went out and happened to things."

Misty and I speak to you from the depths of our heart: Please, please, don't just sit back and let things happen to your relationship. Do something, every day, to make passion happen to your marriage. Bring your personal enthusiasm for connecting, for play, for food, for beauty, for creativity, for health, for God, and for lovemaking into your marriage. If you each bring your most passionate selves to the union of marriage and practice the secrets within these pages, you will fall in love again and again with the same person, day after day, year after year.

I want to close with a memory of a man who lived his whole life with passion, a man I hope to emulate. He was the music man of Ball Avenue, Misty's father, Mike. After he died suddenly in 2012, the chapel filled up, standing room only, for a final honoring and a sweet goodbye. Mike had previously survived two heart attacks, and this last one took his life. I performed the service and prepared as if this were the most important message I would ever give, because it was.

On the day of Mike's funeral, my little boy Solomon stood right with me. At age five, Solomon had written his own eulogy to honor his Pepa. He proudly shared his memories with all gathered. After Solomon spoke, I shared what I knew about this good, loving soul who never had much in the way of material things, but what he had, he always generously shared. I was able to tell the story that Misty's mom, Penny, had told me about the night before he died. Mike had been in a local department store when the lady in front of him realized she didn't have enough money to pay for her purchases. She was searching her purse, and Mike was noticing her dilemma. He did not want to embarrass her by intervening but was compelled to do something. Mike reached into his pocket and pulled out what money he had, then discreetly handed it to the woman with a whisper. "Here, take this to buy your things." She opened her hand and received the gift, confused and smiling, while Mike walked quickly away. He didn't want for her to hesitate or fuss or have to try to say thank you or ask why. He didn't want for her to know his name; he didn't want to receive any kind of glory for his gift. He just wanted this woman to be able to make her purchase and to perhaps feel seen and cared for by a loving, passionate God. Mike never minded walking away empty-handed if he could fill someone else's heart. That's the type of man he was.

Several others at the gathering also shared their memories of Mike. We laughed, nodded our heads, and wiped away tears. Then, in tribute, we filled the chapel with music, his music, and Penny and Misty and her sisters, the husbands and children, all began dancing to one of his favorite records. It was the song he had always played at the end of the "record hops" he would DJ as he made his final call for the last dance: putting needle to vinyl, he would play Jesse Belvin's "Goodnight, My Love."

His life was short, just sixty-seven years, but Mike lived it well, and we still draw on the deep wells of his generous love, his teaching, laughter, and heart. A few days after the funeral, I learned a bit more of his final moments of passion and love, his truly grand finale before leaving this earth. You see, that final night, once he had returned home from his shopping trip, he put on some old records and held Penny in his arms. They laughed and talked about old times, caught up in familiar feelings of romance, remembering how they had started out together as a young couple those forty-eight years prior, and all that had transpired since.

They danced in the living room cheek to cheek, smile to smile. They stayed up all night together, until they finally retired to their bedroom at nearly six in the morning, for the last time. There they made love, a sweet completion after a perfect night of celebrating their bond, their gratitude for each other, and their wholehearted love. And when they finally went to sleep, Mike did not wake again.

Their love had survived hard times, tough spells, and at times difficult kids. Every day presented a struggle of some kind. But their love still endured, grew, and flourished to the end. Mike once said to his wife playfully, "Penny, if you were ever on an airplane that had crashed into a mountain, it wouldn't matter what the news media had reported, I would climb that mountain to go find you for myself to see with my own eyes whether or not you had survived." Penny laughed and nodded knowingly, then immediately replied, "Well, if I had somehow survived a crash like that, I would keep on surviving, 'cause I'd know you'd be coming for me."

Grande amore.

Mike remains in the hearts and memories of us all. He left a great legacy we will pass on to our children and grandchildren. It is a legacy of living with all the passion, mindfulness, and selfless love we can, loving our mates with every drop of energy we have, pursuing their hearts the way God, "the Wild Lover of our souls," passionately pursues us every day of our lives.[1]

If you both are willing to embark on this holy adventure, you too will know a *grande amore.*

> *To love or have loved, that is enough. Ask nothing further. There is no other pearl to be found in the dark folds of life.*
>
> —VICTOR HUGO, *LES MISÉRABLES*

NOTES

Introduction: Monotonous Marriage or a Grande Amore?

1. For more information on how relationships affect aging, here are some fascinating resources: University of North Carolina at Chapel Hill, "Social Networks as Important as Exercise, Diet across the Span of Our Lives: Researchers Show How Social Relationships Reduce Health Risk in Each Stage of Life," *ScienceDaily*, January 4, 2016, www.sciencedaily.com/releases/2016/01/160104163210.htm; Howard S. Friedman and Leslie R. Martin, *The Longevity Project: Surprising Discoveries for Health and Long Life from the Landmark Eight-Decade Study* (New York: Plume, 2012); Dan Buettner, *The Blue Zones: Nine Lessons for Living Longer from the People Who've Lived the Longest*, 2nd ed. (Washington, DC: National Geographic, 2012).

Chapter 1: The Seven Mediterranean Secrets to Passion

1. Marghanita Laski, *Ecstasy: A Study of Some Secular and Religious Experiences* (Westport, Conn.: Greenwood, 1968).

Chapter 2: The Secret of Attunement

1. Sidney M. Jourard, "An Exploratory Study of Body-Accessibility," *British Journal of Social and Clinical Psychology* 5, no. 3 (September 1966): 221–31.
2. Aaron Ben-Zeev, "Why a Lover's Touch Is So Powerful," *Psychology Today*, March 18, 2014, www.psychologytoday.com/blog/in-the-name-love/201405/why-lovers-touch-is-so-powerful.
3. Francesca Di Meglio, "Italian Men: Why Women Can't Get Enough of Them," *Italiansrus.com* (n.d.), www.italiansrus.com/articles/ourpaesani/italianmen.htm.
4. "Italian Men Seduce with Dante at the Beach," August 2003, *Zoomata*, http://archiver.rootsweb.ancestry.com/th/read/ITA-SICILY/2003-08/1061652516.

5. Di Meglio, "Italian Men."
6. Ray Williams, "Eight Reasons Why We Need Human Touch More Than Ever," *Psychology Today*, March 28, 2015, www.psychologytoday.com/blog/wired-success/201503/8-reasons-why-we-need-human-touch-more-ever.
7. Francesca Di Meglio, "Three Winning Tips from Italian Lovers," *Italiansrus.com* (n.d.), www.italiansrus.com/articles/ourpaesani/lovetips.htm.
8. Ibid.
9. Ibid.
10. John Fox, "When Someone Deeply Listens to You," *The Institute for Poetic Medicine*, http://www.poeticmedicine.com/resources-by-john-fox,-cpt.html. (Click "Poetry by John Fox," and then the title of the poem.)

Chapter 3: The Secret of Playfulness

1. "How Did Latomatina Start?" *LaTomatinaTours*, www.latomatinatours.com.
2. Andrea Elyse Messer, "Playfulness May Help Adults Attract Mates, Study Finds," *Penn State News*, August 3, 2012, http://news.psu.edu/story/147649/2012/08/03/playfulness-may-help-adults-attract-mates-study-finds.
3. Ibid.
4. Ibid.
5. "The Spaniard: Everything You Need to Know for Dealing with the Locals," *Just Landed* (n.d.), www.justlanded.com/english/Spain/Spain-Guide/Culture/The-Spaniard.
6. Jodie Gummow, "The Twelve Most Sexually Satisfied Countries," *AlterNet*, February 18, 2014, www.alternet.org/sex-amp-relationships/12-most-sexually-satisfied-countries.
7. Isabel Allende, *Of Love and Shadows*, quoted on www.goodreads.com/quotes/345723-for-women-the-best-aphrodisiacs-are-words-the-g-spot-is.
8. Victoria Woollaston, "Spain's the Place to Live! Spanish Is the Happiest Language in the World—and Its People Are the Most in Love," *Daily Mail Online*, February 13, 2015, www.dailymail.co.uk/sciencetech/article-2952082/Spain-s-place-live-Spanish-happiest-language-world-people-love.html.
9. More information about Cari can be found at www.carijenkins.wordpress.com.

10. Elyssa Garrett, "Eleven Things Americans Could Learn from the Spanish," *Matador Network*, February 24, 2015, http://matadornetwork.com/abroad/11-things-americans-learn-spanish/.

11. "The Spaniard: Everything You Need to Know for Dealing with the Locals," *Just Landed* (n.d.), www.justlanded.com/english/Spain/Spain-Guide/Culture/The-Spaniard.

Chapter 4: The Secret of Savoring Food

1. Elizabeth Bard, *Lunch in Paris: A Love Story, with Recipes* (New York: Little Brown, 2010), 245.

2. Jodie Gummow, "The Twelve Most Sexually Satisfied Countries," *AlterNet*, February 18, 2014, www.alternet.org/sex-amp-relationships/12-most-sexually-satisfied-countries.

3. Matt Bean, "Edible Seduction," *Men's Health*, September 29, 2011, www.menshealth.com/health/edible-seduction.

4. Ibid.

5. Ibid.

6. Samantha Olson, "Foodies and Food Lovers Are Typically Healthier, Engage in More Physical Activity and Adventure," *Medical Daily*, July 7, 2015, www.medicaldaily.com/foodies-and-food-lovers-are-typically-healthier-engage-more-physical-activity-and-341610.

7. Ibid.

8. Kimberly Snyder, "Twenty-Five Foods That Are Natural Aphrodisiacs," *KimberlySnyder.com*, October 3, 2011, http://kimberlysnyder.com/blog/2011/10/03/25-foods-that-are-natural-aphrodisiacs/.

9. Francesca Di Meglio, "Three Winning Tips from Latin Lovers," *Italiansrus.com* (n.d.), http://italiansrus.com/articles/ourpaesani/lovetips_part3.htm.

10. Becky Johnson and Rachel Randolph, *We Laugh, We Cry, We Cook* (Grand Rapids, Mich.: Zondervan, 2013), 134.

11. Paula Butturini, *Keeping the Feast* (New York: Riverhead, 2010), pages 258–59.

12. Johnson and Randolph, *We Laugh, We Cry, We Cook*, 9.

13. Cambria Bold, "Ten Questions to Ask Your Partner at the Dinner Table," *Kitchn*, May 19, 2015, www.thekitchn.com/10-questions-to-ask-your-partner-at-the-dinner-table-219337.

Chapter 5: The Secret of Enjoying Beauty

1. Elizabeth von Arnim, *The Enchanted April* (1922; Charleston: BiblioLife, 2008), 1.
2. Ibid., 58.
3. Ibid.
4. Ibid.
5. Ibid, 59.
6. Emmanuel Stamatakis, Mark Hamer, and David W. Dunstan, "Screen-Based Entertainment Time, All-Cause Mortality, and Cardiovascular Events," vol. 57, no. 3, *Journal of American College of Cardiology* (2011): 292–99.
7. "Spending Time in Nature Makes People Feel More Alive, Study Shows," *University of Rochester*, June 3, 2010, www.rochester.edu/news/show .php?id=3639.

Chapter 6: The Secret of Creativity

1. Ernest Hemingway, *A Movable Feast*, Scribner Classic ed. (1996; New York: Charles Scribner's Sons, 1964), 6.
2. Mihaly Csikszentmihalyi, *Flow: The Psychology of Optimal Experience* (New York: Harper and Row, 1990), 3.
3. Amie Gordon, "Psychology Says Couples Who Play Together Stay Together," *Psych Your Mind*, January 9, 2012, http://psych-your-mind .blogspot.com/2012/01/psychology-says-couples-who-play.html.
4. Bianca P. Acevedo, Arthur Aron, Helen E. Fisher, Lucy L. Brown, "Neural Correlates of Long-Term Intense Romantic Love," *Social Cognitive and Affective Neuroscience* (2012): 7, 145–59.
5. Carolyn Gregoire, "The Psychology of Loves That Last a Lifetime," *Huffington Post*, May 21, 2014, www.huffingtonpost.com/2014/05/21/ psychology-of-lasting-love_n_5339457.html.
6. Ibid.

Chapter 7: The Secret of Health and Longevity

1. Dan Buettner, "The Island Where People Forget to Die," *New York Times Magazine*, October 24, 2012, http://www.nytimes.com/2012/10/28/ magazine/the-island-where-people-forget-to-die.html?_r=0.
2. Material from this section is gleaned from the following resources:

Buettner, "The Island Where People Forget to Die"; Dan Buettner, *The Blue Zones: Nine Lessons for Living Longer from the People Who've Lived the Longest*, 2nd ed., Kindle ed. (Washington, DC: National Geographic, 2012); Anita Sullivan, *Ikaria: A Love Odyssey on a Greek Island* (Amazon Digital Services, 2008); Diane Kochilas, *Ikaria: Lessons on Food, Life, and Longevity from the Greek Island Where People Forget to Die* (Emmaus, Pa.: Rodale, 2014).

3. Buettner, "The Island Where People Forget to Die."
4. Mary Jacobs, "Lessons for a Long Life, from Those Who Live in 'Blue Zones,'" *Dallas Morning News*, May 12, 2014, www.dallasnews.com/real-estate/senior-living/headlines/20140512-lessons-for-a-long-life-from-those-who-live-in-blue-zones.ece.
5. Konstantinos Menzel, "Greece Most Sexually Active Nation, Condom Maker Says," *Greek Reporter.com*, May 20, 2014, http://greece.greekreporter.com/2014/05/30/greece-most-sexually-active-nation/.
6. Ibid.
7. "Greece Ranked among the Most Active and Least Laziest Countries in the World!" *Greek Gateway*, April 26, 2016, www.greekgateway.com/news/greece-ranked-among-the-most-active-and-least-laziest-countries-in-the-world.
8. Anastassios Adamopoulos, "Greeks Have an Average Life Expectancy of 81.4 Years," *Greek Reporter*, November 4, 2015, http://greece.greekreporter.com/2015/11/04/greeks-have-an-average-life-expectancy-of-81-4-years/#sthash.zdiPqqBP.dpuf.
9. Associated Press, "Leaner Nations Bike, Walk, Use Mass Transit," *NBC News*, December 15, 2008, www.nbcnews.com/id/28235890/ns/health-fitness/t/leaner-nations-bike-walk-use-mass-transit/#.VyBHbFYrLIU.
10. "Impact of Daily Exercise on Development of Alzheimer's Disease," *New York Behavioral Health*, May 29, 2013, http://newyorkbehavioralhealth.com/impact-daily-exercise-on-development-alzheimers.
11. Daniel G. Amen, "The Best Anti-Aging Secret," August 20, 2015, http://danielamenmd.com/best-anti-aging-secret/.
12. Ozzie Jacobs, "Effect of Exercise on Sex Drive," *Livestrong*, June 24, 2015, www.livestrong.com/article/80273-effect-exercise-sex-drive/.
13. Ibid.
14. Deborah Dunham, "Could Exercise Be Your Key to Happily Ever After?"

Youbeauty, May 9, 2012, www.youbeauty.com/aha/exercise-improves -relationships/.

15. Ibid.

16. Ibid.

17. Ibid.

Chapter 8: The Secret of Blending the Sacred and the Sexual

1. Sabrina Bachai, "Top Ten Reasons Why Sex Is Good for You," *Medical Daily*, May 20, 2013, www.medicaldaily.com/top-10-reasons-why-sex -good-you-246020.

2. Tracey R. Rich, "Kosher Sex," *Judaism 101*, www.jewfaq.org/sex.htm.

3. Earl Henslin, *This Is Your Brain in Love* (Nashville: Thomas Nelson, 2010), 21.

4. Shmuley Boteach, *The Kosher Sutra: Eight Sacred Secrets for Reigniting Desire and Restoring Passion for Life* (New York: Harper One, 2009), 107.

Conclusion: Personal Parting Thoughts

1. John Eldredge and Brent Curtis wrote a powerful classic, *The Sacred Romance* (Nashville: Thomas Nelson, 2001), about God's passionate pursuit of us, describing God as a Wild Lover who will settle for nothing less than our whole hearts. Highly recommended.

ABOUT
STEPHEN ARTERBURN

Stephen Arterburn is the founder and chairman of New Life Ministries and host of the number-one nationally syndicated Christian-counseling talk show *New Life Live!* heard and watched by more than two million people each week on nearly two hundred radio stations nation-wide, on XM and Sirius Satellite radio, and on the NRBTV television network. He is also the founder and creator of Women of Faith, with conferences attended by more than five million women. Additionally, he serves as teaching pastor at Northview Church in Carmel, Indiana.

Steve also hosts New Life TV, a web-based channel dedicated to transforming lives through God's truth. Steve is a nationally and interna-tionally known public speaker and has been featured in national media venues such as *Oprah, Inside Edition, Good Morning America, CNN Live, The New York Times, USA Today, US News and World Report, ABC World News Tonight,* and, ironically, in *GQ* and *Rolling Stone* magazines. Steve has spoken at major events for the National Center for Fathering, American Association of Christian Counselors, Promise Keepers Canada, Life Well Conferences in Australia, and The Salvation Army, to name a few.

Stephen Arterburn is a bestselling and award-winning author with more than ten million books in print. He has authored and co-authored books such as *Every Man's Battle, Healing Is a Choice,* and his latest books, *Take Your Life Back, Take Your Life Back Day by Day,* and the *Twelve Gifts of Life Recovery.* He has been nominated for numerous writing awards and has won three Gold Medallions for writing excellence. Steve has created and edited ten study and specialty Bibles, including, along with Dr. Stoop, the number-one-selling *Life Recovery Bible.*

His speaking topics address issues common to leaders and adult men and women, including *Every Man's Battle*, *Lose It for Life*, *Is This the One?*, *Toxic Faith*, *Take Your Life Back*, and *Every Man a Leader*.

Steve has degrees from Baylor University and the University of North Texas, as well as two honorary doctorate degrees. Steve resides with his family in Fishers, Indiana.

ABOUT NEW LIFE MINISTRIES

New Life Ministries, founded by Stephen Arterburn, began in 1988 as New Life Treatment Centers. New Life's nationally broadcast radio program, *New Life Live!*, began in early 1995. Women of Faith conferences, also founded by Stephen Arterburn, began in 1996. New Life's Counselor Network was formed in 2000, and TV.NewLife.com, our internet-based television channel, was launched in 2014.

The Mission of New Life is to "transform lives through compassionately communicating God's truth and connecting people into redemptive relationships."

New Life Ministries is a nationally recognized, faith-based, broadcasting and counseling nonprofit organization providing ministry through radio, TV, our counseling network, workshops, support groups, and numerous written, audio, and video resources. All New Life resources are based on God's truth and help those who are hurting find and build connections and experience life transformation.

Our *New Life Live!* radio program, still the centerpiece of our ministry, is broadcast on Christian radio stations in more than 150 markets, including most major metropolitan areas and XM/SIRIUS satellite radio. *New Life Live!* can also be seen on NRB, SkyAngel, and The WalkTV, as well as our internet-based television channel.

Our passion is to reach out compassionately to those seeking emotional and spiritual health and healing for God's glory. New Life Ministries Resource Center receives thousands of calls each month from those looking to us for help. We look forward to the future with hope that God will continue to bless our ministry and those we serve.

www.newlife.com

Is This the One?
Insightful Dates for Finding the Love of Your Life

Stephen Arterburn, M.ED.

Who to marry.

Who to leave behind.

The skyrocketing divorce rate seems to suggest that "no regrets" marriages are impossible. Award-winning author Stephen Arterburn begs to differ.

Arterburn maintains that the key to a long-term, happy relationship is making sure you're taking the plunge with the right person.

Rather than aiming at marriages already in jeopardy, Arterburn focuses attention on the beginning of relationships—before the commitment and deep emotional investment, before the chaos and anger of a failing marriage. He prescribes three sets of ten carefully devised dates designed specifically to help couples reveal their true colors, clarify their priorities, and honestly assess their compatibility.

According to Arterburn, great marriages require hard work. What's more—and if you're looking for the message of this book in a nutshell, you've found it—marriages that last are the product of better decision-making before couples say "I do."

Spiritually sound and street-smart, *Is This the One?* offers a practical, insightful, fun strategy for making a relationship choice you can live with. Forever.

NIV, Spiritual Renewal Study Bible, Hardcover

Experience New Growth and Transformation in Your Spiritual Walk

Stephen Arterburn and David Stoop

Are you experiencing a hunger to know God more completely in your life? Do you long for a deeper connection with him? If so, then the *NIV Spiritual Renewal Bible*—the recipient of the 1999 ECPA Gold Medallion Award—is for you. Using a time-tested process honed over decades of counseling and teaching, Stephen Arterburn employs seven core principles of spiritual renewal and refreshment, connecting you more closely with God's Spirit through his Word and helping you to develop the deep, satisfying change you desire in your spiritual life.

Features:

- Sixty-six book introductions focus on the thematic study and spiritual renewal aspects of each Bible book.

- Text notes highlight renewal themes as they emerge from the text of the Bible.

- Multifeature character profiles assess how different personalities managed different challenges in their walk with God.

- Spiritual keys devotional reading plan: two cycles (OT and NT) of forty-nine devotions each lead the reader through seven keys of spiritual renewal with seven devotions for each key.

- Spiritual disciplines essays describe the various disciplines of the faith, such as prayer, Scripture reading, and others.

- Spiritual disciplines profiles: one-page articles describe how certain characters of the Bible employed the various spiritual disciplines in their lives.

Available in stores and online!